Zakariya year 5-F

Zakariya Yow 5-1

I LOVE ISLAM

International Edition

5

ISLAMIC STUDIES TEXTBOOK SERIES - LEVEL FIVE

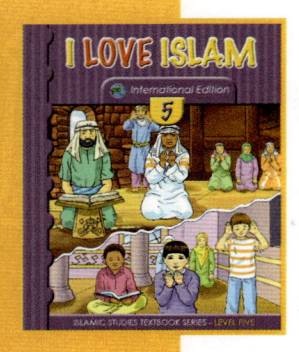

I Love Islam 5

International Edition

I Love Islam © is a series of Islamic Studies textbooks that gradually introduces Muslim students to the essentials of their faith. It brings to light the historic and cultural aspects of Islam. The series covers levels one through five, which are suitable for young learners and includes a student textbooks and workbooks as well as a teacher and parent's guides.

The Islamic Services Foundation is undertaking this project in collaboration with Brighter Horizons Academy in Dallas, Texas. Extensive efforts have been made to review the enclosed material. However, constructive suggestions and comments that would enrich the content of this work are welcome.

All praise is due to Allah (God), for providing us with the resources that have enabled us to complete the first part of this series. This is an ongoing project, and it is our sincere wish and hope that it will impact our Muslim children today, and for many years to come.

Copyright © 2015 by Islamic Services Foundation

ISBN 1-933301-39-6

All rights reserved. No part of this publication may be reproduced or transmitted in any form or by any means, electronic or mechanical, including photocopying, recording, or any information storage and retrieval system, without permission in writing from the publisher.

PROGRAM DIRECTOR *

Nabil Sadoun, Ed.D.

WRITING TEAM

Ummukulthum Al-Maawiy
Lena Dirbashi
Nabil Sadoun, Ed.D.

REVIEWERS AND ADVISORS

Susan Douglass
Freda Shamma, Ph.D.

CONTRIBUTORS

Suad Abu Amarah
Sumayah Al-Khatib
Kacem Ayachi
Romana El-Rouby
Nicholas Howard
Sandra Schaffer
Omar Tarazi
Menat Zihni

CURRICULUM DESIGN

Nabil Sadoun, Ed.D.
Majida Salem

GRAPHIC DESIGN

Mohammed Eid Mubarak

ILLUSTRATIONS

Raed Abdulwahid
Special thanks to: Goodword Books

PHOTOGRAPHY

Al-Anwar Designs

PUBLISHER AND OWNER

ISF PUBLICATIONS

Islamic Services Foundation
P.O. Box 451623
Garland, Texas 75045
U.S.A
Tel: +1 972-414-5090
Fax: +1 972-414-5640
www.myislamicbooks.com

* Names are in alphabetical order of the last names.

UNIT A — Tawheed: The Faith of All Prophets

CHAPTER 1	Prophets of Islam	A2
CHAPTER 2	Prophets and messengers	A12
CHAPTER 3	Tawheed: The Faith of All Prophets	A22
CHAPTER 4	Away From Tawheed	A32
CHAPTER 5	Surat-un-Naba':	A46
Lesson 1	Surat-un-Naba': 1	A46
Lesson 2	Surat-un-Naba': 2	A48
Lesson 3	Surat-un-Naba': 3	A50

UNIT B — MANY PROPHETS, ONE GOD

CHAPTER 1	Prophet Hud	B2
CHAPTER 2	Prophet Salih	B12
CHAPTER 3	Prophet Lut and the People of Sodom	B22
CHAPTER 4	Turning to Allah: The Story Of Prophet Younus	B34

UNIT C — MUSLIMS UNDER SIEGE

CHAPTER 1	Disobedience is Harmful: The Battle of Uhud	C2
CHAPTER 2	Searching for the Truth: The Journey of Salman Al-Farisi	C12
CHAPTER 3	Surat-ut-takweer :	C20
Lesson 1	Surat-ut-takweer 1	C20
Lesson 2	Surat-ut-takweer 2	C22

UNIT D — WORSHIP WITH HEART

CHAPTER 1	Al Khushoo' the Heart of Worship	D2
CHAPTER 2	Salat-ul-Jama'ah: A Prayer Allah loves	D10
CHAPTER 3	How To Pray Salat-ul-Jama'ah	D16
CHAPTER 4	Salat-ul-Jumu'ah: The Friday Prayer	D22
CHAPTER 5	Appreciating Allah's Gifts	D30
CHAPTER 6	Sujood-ush-Shukr	D38
CHAPTER 7	Zakah: The Third Pillar of Islam	D46

UNIT E — MY ISLAMIC CHARACTER

CHAPTER 1	Brotherhood in Islam	E2
CHAPTER 2	Muslims Love Each Other	E8
CHAPTER 3	The Six Rights of Muslims on One Another	E14
CHAPTER 4	Helping Others, Helping Yourself	E22
CHAPTER 5	I Do Not Hurt Others	E30
CHAPTER 6	Surat-ul-Mutaffifeen :	E38
Lesson 1	Surat-ul-Mutaffifeen 1	E38
Lesson 1	Surat-ul-Mutaffifeen 2	E40

UNIT F — ISLAMIC LIFE STYLE

CHAPTER 1	Muslim Fashion	F2
CHAPTER 2	Muslims Online	F8

"I Love Islam" Friends and Family

- Zaid
- Leena
- Mr. Mahmood
- Mrs. Mahmood
- Bilal
- Sarah
- Mr. Siraj
- Mrs. Siraj
- Amir
- Omar
- Mona
- Khalid
- Ahmad
- Teacher Hibah
- Baby Yousuf

UNIT A

Tawheed: The Faith of All Prophets

CHAPTER 1	Prophets of Islam	A2
CHAPTER 2	Prophets and messengers	A12
CHAPTER 3	Tawheed: The Faith of All Prophets	A22
CHAPTER 4	Away From Tawheed	A32
CHAPTER 5	Surat-ul-Naba':	A46
LESSON 1	Surat-ul-Naba' 1	A46
LESSON 2	Surat-ul-Naba' 2	A48
LESSON 3	Surat-ul-Naba' 3	A50

A1

UNIT A

CHAPTER ONE

Prophets of Islam

Pre-reading Questions

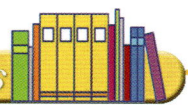

1. What is the main message of all prophets?
2. Were the prophets ordinary men?
3. What are the characteristics of prophets?
4. What were some of the miracles our prophets brought with them?
5. Are the prophets mentioned in the Qur'an similar to those mentioned in the Bible?
6. Who was the last and final prophet?
7. How should we respect our prophets?

Introduction

As you learned earlier, the concept of tawheed (monotheism) is the most important concept in Islam. The key to Heaven is to understand and believe that there is no God but Allah, the One True Creator. Allah wanted the message of Islam and the belief in one God, 'tawheed,' to spread among mankind. He did this by appointing prophets and messengers.

Allah Sent Prophets to All Nations

Islam teaches that God sent prophets and messengers to all nations. Since the beginning of time, God has communicated His guidance through these chosen people. They were human beings who walked and lived among their people. They taught nations about faith in One Almighty God and how to be good. From the first prophet, Adam (P), to the last prophet, Muhammad ﷺ, Allah's message eventually reached all corners of the world. Allah says in the Qur'an:

﴿ وَلِكُلِّ أُمَّةٍ رَسُولٌ ﴾ يونس: ٤٧

"And for every nation there is a messenger." [10:47]

﴿ إِنَّا أَرْسَلْنَاكَ بِالْحَقِّ بَشِيرًا وَنَذِيرًا وَإِن مِّنْ أُمَّةٍ إِلَّا خَلَا فِيهَا نَذِيرٌ ﴾ فاطر: ٢٤

"Indeed we have sent with you the truth conveying to people Our good tidings and warnings. And there is no nation, which has not been sent a warning (messenger of warning)." [35:24]

The Qur'an itself tells us that it has mentioned only some of the prophets:

﴿ وَرُسُلًا قَدْ قَصَصْنَاهُمْ عَلَيْكَ مِن قَبْلُ وَرُسُلًا لَّمْ نَقْصُصْهُمْ عَلَيْكَ ﴾ النساء: ١٦٤

"And we told you about some messengers, while we did not tell you about others." [4:164]

Since prophets appeared over thousands of years, and there were many in each nation, to make a full list of names is impossible. There are some ahadeeth of the Prophet which say that God sent thousands of prophets and messengers. Therefore, Muslims have to believe in and respect all the prophets that are mentioned in Al-Qur'an. And, they should also believe that Allah sent many other prophets and messengers whose names are not known. The Holy Qur'an stated:

Words of Wisdom — Holy Qur'an

﴿ ءَامَنَ الرَّسُولُ بِمَا أُنزِلَ إِلَيْهِ مِن رَّبِّهِ وَالْمُؤْمِنُونَ كُلٌّ ءَامَنَ بِاللَّهِ وَمَلَائِكَتِهِ وَكُتُبِهِ وَرُسُلِهِ لَا نُفَرِّقُ بَيْنَ أَحَدٍ مِّن رُّسُلِهِ ﴾ البقرة: ٢٨٥

"The Messenger (Muhammad) believes in what has been revealed to him from his Lord, as do the men of faith. Each one (of them) believes in Allah, His angels, His books, and His messengers. We make no distinction (they say) between one and another of His messengers." [2:285]

UNIT A CHAPTER 1

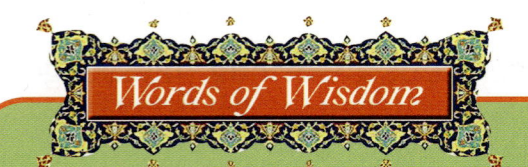

Words of Wisdom

Hadeeth Shareef

عن أبي وهب الجشمي قال: قال رسول الله ﷺ قال:
"تَسَمَّوا بأَسْماءِ الأنبياءِ، وأَحبُّ الأَسْماءِ إلى اللهِ: عبد الله وعبد الرحمن."
رواه أبو داود والنسائي وأحمد

Abu Wahm Al-Jashmi narrated that rasoolullah ﷺ said: "Choose the names of prophets for yourselves. And the names that Allah loves the most are Abdullah and Abdur-Rahman."
Reported in Abu Dawood, Nasa'i and Ahmad.

All Prophets were Human Beings

Prophets and messengers were human beings who were very noble and pious role models. They were neither divine, nor angels nor jinn. Every prophet was born to a mother and a father, except Prophet Isa عليه السلام, who had no father, and Adam عليه السلام who had neither. Some prophets had brothers like Prophet Musa عليه السلام. Prophet Musa's brother was also a prophet, and his name was Haroon عليه السلام. Ismaeel and Ishaq were also brothers and prophets. Other prophets got married and had children, like Prophets Adam, Nuh, Ibraheem, Musa, Muhammad ﷺ and others. Although prophets and messengers were ordinary men, Allah ﷻ gave them special qualities. They all had high morals, manners and attitudes. They were faithful, honest, patient, tolerant, and honorable. Additionally, some of them had long lives. Prophet Nuh عليه السلام lived for 950 years and Prophet Ibraheem lived more than 200 years! Other prophets died much younger than that, such as Prophet Muhammad ﷺ. He became a prophet at the age of 40 and died at the age of 63. Prophet Isa عليه السلام is the only prophet who has yet to die. Instead, Allah ﷻ raised him to Heaven. He will come back to Earth before the Day of Judgment, and he will confirm Islam as the true and final religion of God. He will also win over all evil people and powers.

All Prophets were Men

Being a prophet or a messenger was not an easy task. It was a very serious responsibility, which required a great deal of perseverance and strength. Some prophets were killed, like Prophets Zakariyya (Zachariah) and Yahya (John) عليه السلام. Others were put in prison for years, like Prophet Yousuf (Joseph). Almost all prophets were persecuted and harassed, including Nuh (Noah), Ibraheem عليه السلام (Abraham), Younus (Jonah), Musa (Moses), Isa (Jesus), Muhammad, and others. Therefore, Allah in His glorious wisdom carefully selected those individuals who would be most suited to serve as prophets. Allah also stated that he chose only men to be prophets and messengers.

Words of Wisdom — Holy Qur'an

﴿ وَمَا أَرْسَلْنَا مِن قَبْلِكَ إِلَّا رِجَالًا نُّوحِىٓ إِلَيْهِم مِّنْ أَهْلِ ٱلْقُرَىٰ ﴾ يوسف: ١٠٩

And We have not sent before you but men from (among) the people of the towns, to whom We sent revelations. [12:109]

However, Allah chose certain faithful women to play great and historical roles. Asiah, the wife of Phir'oun, Maryam, Khadeejah and many others were exceptional role models. They were not prophets, but they were women of great faith.

The Message of Prophethood

▲ *The Cave of Hira, where Prophet Muhammad recieved the first verses of Al-Qur'an.*

▲ *Mount Sinai, where Prophet Musa received the Torah.*

A5

How did prophets find out that they had been selected as prophets or messengers? There were two ways in which Allah ﷻ reached out to his prophets. The first way was by sending an angel to them. For example, Prophet Muhammad ﷺ received the message of prophethood from the Angel Jibreel while he was in Cave Hiraa'.

At other times, Allah ﷻ spoke directly to His chosen prophets. For example, Prophet Musa عليه السلام went to a desert or a mountain where Allah ﷻ spoke to him directly.

All the prophets received the same basic message: That Allah is the only true Creator and Sustainer of the universe, and that He is the only One worthy of complete obedience and worship. Adam, Nuh, Ibraheem, Musa, Isa, Muhammad, and all the prophets brought their people this same message. None of them claimed to be divine or God-like in any way, and they all taught a pure belief in the One True God.

Characteristics of Prophets

What Are The Characteristics of Prophets?

1. The prophets of Allah were the best in their communities. They were the most moral and the most intelligent among their peoples. This was necessary because the life of a prophet served as a model for his followers. His personality had to be pleasant in order to attract people towards his message rather than drive them away.

﴿ وَإِنَّكَ لَعَلَىٰ خُلُقٍ عَظِيمٍ ﴾ القلم: ٤

"And most surely you are of a great moral character." [68:4]

2. They usually came from well-known and highly respected families. Most prophets came from great lineage. Prophets Musa, Haroon, Yousuf, and Yaqoub were the offspring of Prophet Ibraheem, the Father of Prophets, through his son Is'haq. Prophet Muhammad was the descendent of Prophet Isma'eel. Isma'eel was also the son of Prophet Ibraheem.

3. Prophets had to possess strong personalities. They had to be strong and resilient in the face of challenges and difficulties. Many Prophets had to face fierce and evil enemies.

4. Prophets had to be patient and tolerant. Each prophet had to bring the message of tawheed to his people and teach this message for many, many years. Many prophets, including Prophet Muhammad ﷺ were persecuted and ridiculed for

teaching Allah's message. Others, like Nuh, taught for hundreds of years, but only gained a few followers. In the case of Prophet Younus, the persecution and harassment got so bad that he fled, abandoning the people whom he was supposed to teach.

Prophets and Miracles

Allah ﷻ provided some of His prophets with miracles. These miracles usually had one of two purposes:

- To help them during times of danger or trouble (Prophet Ibraheem, Nuh, Younus)
- Or as proof of Allah's greatness and to prove that the prophet is a true prophet. (Prophet Musa, Isa, etc.)

Prophet Ibraheem عليه السلام was saved from the huge fire that was lit to burn him. Prophet Nuh عليه السلام was miraculously saved with his family and followers from the flood.

The nature of the miracles depended upon the time and society in which the prophet taught. Allah knew that people would be most impressed by miracles that accomplished valued tasks in society. So, He chose miracles that would be relevant to the society of His messengers. For example, Moses' contemporaries were excellent at magic. So his major miracle was to defeat the best magicians of the day in Egypt. Jesus' contemporaries were recognized as skillful physicians. Therefore, his miracles were to raise the dead and cure the incurable diseases. The Arabs, the contemporaries of the Prophet Muhammad ﷺ, were known for their eloquence and magnificent poetry. So Prophet Muhammad's ﷺ major miracle was Al-Qur'an. The people of Arabia were impressed by the eloquence of Al-Qur'an and Arab poets and orators could not make even a few verses like it. Later, all Arabia became a Muslim nation.

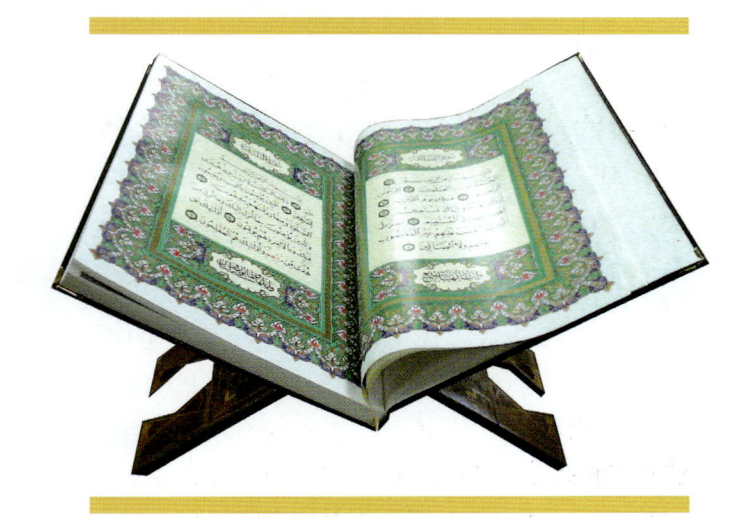

Prophets in the Bible

There are 25 prophets mentioned by name in the Qur'an, although Allah tells us clearly that there were many more in different times and places. Christians and Jews also believe in most of the same prophets and their miracles. Provided here are the 25 mentioned in the Qur'an and their English names from the Bible where applicable:

	Qur'anic Name	Biblical Name
1	Adam	Adam
2	Idrees	Enoch
3	Nuh	Noah
4	Hud	-----
5	Salih	-----
6	Ibraheem	Abraham
7	Isma'eel	Ishmael
8	Is-haq	Isaac
9	Loot	Lot
10	Ya'qoob	Jacob
11	Yousuf	Joseph
12	Shu'ayb	Jethro
13	Ayyoob	Job
14	Musa	Moses
15	Haroon	Aaron
16	Thul-kifl	Ezekiel
17	Dawood	David
18	Sulayman	Solomon
19	Ilyas	Elias
20	Al-Yasa'	Elisha
21	Younus	Jonah
22	Zakariyya	Zecharias
23	Yahya	John
24	'Isa	Jesus
25	Muhammad	-----

As you can see, most of the prophets in the Qur'an are recognized by the Bible. Some of the prophets have the same name in both the Qur'an and the Bible, like Prophet Adam عليه السلام. However, most prophets have names which sound different. For example, Prophet Sulayman عليه السلام is known as Prophet Solomon in the English translation of the Bible. Prophet Younus عليه السلام is known as Prophet Jonah. Also, Prophet Ayyoub is known as Job.

There are some prophets mentioned in the Qur'an that are not mentioned in the existing form of the Bible. For example Prophets Muhammad ﷺ, Shu'ayb عليه السلام, Salih and Hud عليه السلام.

Respecting our Prophets

1. Believing in all of the true prophets and admiring them is a Muslim's way of showing appreciation. Muslims appreciate the many sacrifices that these prophets made. We must be grateful that they worked so hard to bring Allah's message to mankind.

2. The best way to respect prophets and messengers is to follow their guidance and manners. If you want to give great respect to Prophet Muhammad, for example, you must obey him and try to follow his manners and Sunnah.

3. When Muslims mention the name of Prophet Muhammad or any other prophet, they make a prayer for them out of respect. This is a prayer asking God to grant the prophet His peace and blessings. In Arabic we say:

عليه السلام or صلى الله عليه وسلم

"Sallallahu alayhi wasallam or

▲ *The Tomb of Prophet Yahya (John) عليه السلام in the Omayyad Mosque in Damascas, Syria.*

Alayhi-ssalam"

4. Muslims do not draw pictures of the prophets. In addition, Muslims do not portray the characters of the prophets in movies or plays. Muslims believe that portraying a prophet of God in a movie is disrespectful. No matter how good an artist or an actor is, it would be impossible for them to accurately portray the prophet's greatness. Also, Muslims do not

A9

want to create images of prophets as other groups have done, because that could lead to idolizing those images. People in the past used to create statues of their great leaders, then ended up worshipping them.

That is why we do not see any actor playing Prophet Muhammad in the famous movie "The Message." And even in the animated movie "Muhammad: The Last Messenger," no image of the Prophet is ever depicted.

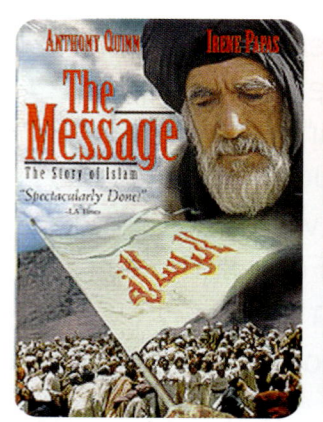

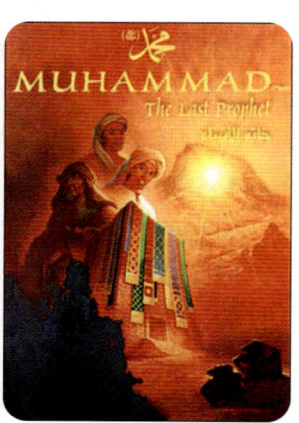

Healthy Habits

1. Always show love and respect for all the prophets of Allah.

2. Always follow the Sunnah and manners of Prophet Muhammad.

3. Say "Salla-Allahu Alayhi wa Sallam" or "Alay-his-Salam" whenever you hear or say the name of Prophet Muhammad or other prophets.

Chapter Review

Think Critically

Why do you think Allah chose humans, not angels, for example, to be prophets and messengers?

Lesson Review

1. What does Islam teach about prophets? Quote two verses from the Qur'an.

2. How many prophets are mentioned in the Holy Qur'an?

3. Explain how prophets were ordinary men. Why did Allah choose these individuals?

4. What were two ways in which these ordinary men learned that they were prophets?

5. Why did Allah ﷻ provide some of His prophets with miracles?

6. What are some of the characteristics of a prophet?

7. Which prophets are not mentioned by name in today's Bible?

8. What are the English Biblical names for Prophets Younus, Dawood, Yahya Thul-Kifl, Ayyoub and Ya'qoub?

9. What is the significance of Prophet Muhammad ﷺ?

10. List three ways Muslims can show respect to the prophets.

UNIT A

Prophets and messengers

CHAPTER TWO

Introduction

Prophets and messengers were great people selected by Allah to show people the straight path. They came from different places and spoke different languages, but they all conveyed the same message of Islam. They all focused on the most important concept of Islam, tawheed. Some of them were anbiyaa', or prophets, and others were rusul, or messengers.

Word Watch

[Prophet: Nabiy نبي
Prophets: Anbiyaa' أنبياء
Messenger: rasool رسول
messengers: Rusul رُسُل]

Many messengers, One Message

After the creation of Adam, just one original message has been repeatedly delivered to mankind throughout the history of humanity. All prophets taught their peoples about the oneness of Allah, or Tawheed, and the proper way to worship Him. They also taught people how to be righteous and lead positive and happy lives. Allah's message has been the same message from the first prophet, Adam to the last prophet, Muhammad ﷺ.

God gave them all His guidance and charged them with the task of conveying that guidance to His people. The Prophet's ﷺ mission was to encourage people to believe in the One True God, obey Him, do good, and avoid evil.

In Surat-ul-A'raaf, Allah tells us that although He sent different prophets to different peoples in different times, they all had the same message, "God is One, and He is the only One to worship."

Words of Wisdom

Holy Qur'an

﴿ لَقَدْ أَرْسَلْنَا نُوحًا إِلَىٰ قَوْمِهِ فَقَالَ يَٰقَوْمِ اعْبُدُوا۟ ٱللَّهَ مَا لَكُم مِّنْ إِلَٰهٍ غَيْرُهُۥٓ إِنِّىٓ أَخَافُ عَلَيْكُمْ عَذَابَ يَوْمٍ عَظِيمٍ ﴾ الأعراف: ٥٩

We sent Nuh to his people. He said: "O my people! Worship Allah! You have no other god but Him. Truly I fear for you the punishment of painful day." [7:59]

﴿ وَإِلَىٰ عَادٍ أَخَاهُمْ هُودًا ۗ قَالَ يَٰقَوْمِ اعْبُدُوا۟ ٱللَّهَ مَا لَكُم مِّنْ إِلَٰهٍ غَيْرُهُۥٓ أَفَلَا تَتَّقُونَ ﴾ الأعراف: ٦٥

To the people of Aad, (We sent) Hud, one of their (own) brethren. He said: "O my people! Worship Allah! You have no other God but Him, will you not, then, seek protection." [7:65]

﴿ وَإِلَىٰ ثَمُودَ أَخَاهُمْ صَٰلِحًا ۗ قَالَ يَٰقَوْمِ اعْبُدُوا۟ ٱللَّهَ مَا لَكُم مِّنْ إِلَٰهٍ غَيْرُهُۥ ﴾ الأعراف: ٧٣

To the people of Thamood (We sent) Salih, one of their own brethren. He said: "O my people! Worship Allah; you have no other god but Him." [7:73]

﴿ وَإِلَىٰ مَدْيَنَ أَخَاهُمْ شُعَيْبًا ۗ قَالَ يَٰقَوْمِ اعْبُدُوا۟ ٱللَّهَ مَا لَكُم مِّنْ إِلَٰهٍ غَيْرُهُۥ ﴾ الأعراف: ٨٥

To the people of Madyan, We sent Shu'ayb, one of their own brethren, he said: "O my people! Worship Allah; you have no other god but Him." [7:85]

﴿ وَمَآ أَرْسَلْنَا مِن قَبْلِكَ مِن رَّسُولٍ إِلَّا نُوحِىٓ إِلَيْهِ أَنَّهُۥ لَآ إِلَٰهَ إِلَّآ أَنَا۠ فَٱعْبُدُونِ ﴾ الأنبياء: ٢٥

Not a messenger did We send before thee without this inspiration sent by Us to him: that there is no God but I; therefore worship and serve Me. [21:25]

Allah, The One True Creator

Prophets	The Message
Adam	God is One
Nuh	God is One
Abraham	God is One
Moses	God is One
Jesus	God is One
Muhammad	God is One

A13

The Difference Between Prophets and messengers

The terms "prophets" and "messengers" are sometimes used as if they always mean the same thing. This is not the case all of the time. All prophets shared one common message, Islam. And all prophets were required to implement Islam in their own lives and guide their families too. However, some of the prophets were also messengers. Those messengers were ordered by Allah to deliver Allah's message to many other people.

A rasool means a person who is assigned to deliver Allah's message to the people of his tribe or in his area. The rasool, then, is a prophet whom Allah ordered to guide a large number of people to worshipping God and practicing Islam. This was a very important role given to messengers in addition to the responsibilities of prophethood.

Of the many prophets Allah ﷻ sent, only 25 are mentioned by name in the Qur'an. All of them were messengers except Prophet Adam. He lived alone on Earth with his small family. Therefore, he was not ordered to convey Allah's message outside of his family. All the other prophets mentioned in the Qur'an from Nuh to Muhammad were rusul, or messengers. It should be noted here that Prophet Nuh was the first of Allah's messengers.

Contrasting Prophets and Messengers

Description	Prophets	messengers
Great people	*	*
Human beings	*	*
Men	*	*
Given divine messages	*	*
Must deliver the message to many other people		*
Perhaps given books		*

CORRECTION

Many people think that messengers are only those who received books from God. That is not true. There are messengers who did not receive books. Allah said in the Qur'an that Prophets Isma'eel, Lut, Yousuf, Ilyas, Younus, Salih, Hud and others are rusul, or messengers, although they did not receive books. Look at the following ayaat:

﴿ وَاذْكُرْ فِي ٱلْكِتَٰبِ إِسْمَٰعِيلَ إِنَّهُۥ كَانَ صَادِقَ ٱلْوَعْدِ وَكَانَ رَسُولًا نَّبِيًّا ﴾ مريم: ٥٤

And mention Isma'eel in the Book; surely he was truthful in (his) promise, and he was a messenger, a prophet. [19:54]

﴿ وَإِنَّ إِلْيَاسَ لَمِنَ ٱلْمُرْسَلِينَ ﴾ الصافات: ١٢٣

And Ilyas was most surely one of the messengers. [37:123]

﴿ وَإِنَّ لُوطًا لَّمِنَ ٱلْمُرْسَلِينَ ﴾ الصافات: ١٣٣

And Lut was most surely one of the messengers. [37:133]

﴿ وَإِنَّ يُونُسَ لَمِنَ ٱلْمُرْسَلِينَ ﴾ الصافات: ١٣٩

And Younus was most surely one of the messengers. [37:139]

The role of a messenger

The main role of the messenger is to convey the message of Allah to his people. Allah says:

﴿ مَّا عَلَى ٱلرَّسُولِ إِلَّا ٱلۡبَلَٰغُ ﴾ آل عمران: ٨١

"The Messenger's duty is but to convey (the Message)..." [3:81]

Allah also says:
"O Apostle! Proclaim the (Message) which has been sent to you from your Lord. If you do not, you will not have fulfilled (your obligation) and taught His message." [5:67]

As you learned earlier, messengers were given the responsibility of teaching their people Islam. Each messenger was only responsible for conveying Allah's message to his people. They were not responsible for bringing the message to people outside of their areas, unless Allah ordered them to do so. The situation of Prophet Muhammad was different. He was sent as a messenger and guide for his people and for all of humankind. Allah says:

﴿ وَمَآ أَرۡسَلۡنَٰكَ إِلَّا كَآفَّةً لِّلنَّاسِ بَشِيرًا وَنَذِيرًا وَلَٰكِنَّ أَكۡثَرَ ٱلنَّاسِ لَا يَعۡلَمُونَ ﴾ سبأ: ٢٨

"We have not sent you but as a universal (Messenger) to mankind, giving them glad tidings, and warning them (against sin), but most people do not understand." [34:28]

During his 23 years as a messenger, he taught the people of Arabia the message of Islam, and all of Arabia became a Muslim nation. Before he died, he sent his ambassadors with messages to the kings of Persia, the Roman Empire, Egypt, and other nations outside of Arabia inviting them to Islam. Some of these nations, as well as others not mentioned, accepted Islam after the passing of Prophet Muhammad ﷺ.

messengers are sent to:
1. Teach Allah's message of faith
2. Teach people how to worship their Creator
3. Show people how to live moral and happy lives.

▲ *The Prophet's Mosque in Madinah*

Prophet Muhammad ﷺ: The Final Prophet and Messenger

All prophets were chosen by God, and their messages were equally true. However, their missions varied. The messengers before the Prophet Muhammad ﷺ were only given teachings for their nations. During those times, except for trade or war, nations didn't interact with each other. Furthermore, the teachings of each prophet lasted for a limited time, after which God would send another prophet to revise some of the teachings for the new circumstances.

But eventually the time came to unite all nations with a single religion. Allah wanted humankind to live in peace as one nation. For this purpose God sent Prophet Muhammad ﷺ to all mankind. Allah entrusted him to deliver His teachings to the whole world and for eternity. This teaching is Islam in its complete form.

Prophet Muhammad's ﷺ mission was to confirm the basic teachings of Islam that other prophets had taught. He also came with many additional teachings and guidance for the good of mankind. Islam as we know it now is a comprehensive and perfect way of life. If people follow this guidance, they will live happily in this life, and win the wonderful Paradise in the after life.

Prophet Muhammad ﷺ is the final Prophet and Messenger. He brought us the final message from God, the Qur'an. No true prophet or messenger will come after Prophet Muhammad, and no divine message will come after Al-Qur'an. Allah says in Al-Qur'an:

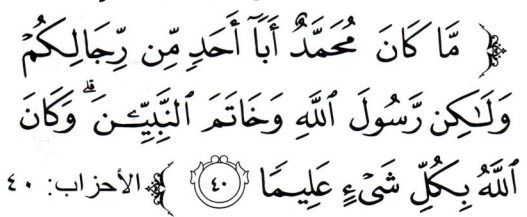

﴿ مَّا كَانَ مُحَمَّدٌ أَبَآ أَحَدٍ مِّن رِّجَالِكُمْ وَلَٰكِن رَّسُولَ ٱللَّهِ وَخَاتَمَ ٱلنَّبِيِّۦنَ وَكَانَ ٱللَّهُ بِكُلِّ شَىْءٍ عَلِيمًا ﴾ الأحزاب: ٤٠

"Muhammad is not the father of any of your men, but he is the Messenger of Allah and the Last of the Prophets; and Allah is knowledgeable of all things." [33:40]

Al-Qur'an's message confirms but replaces all former holy books and scriptures that people changed or were lost over time.

▲ *Inside the Prophet's Mosque in Madinah*

Anyone who claims to be a prophet after Prophet Muhammad ﷺ is a false prophet. And any claimed divine message after the Qur'an is not from God.

It is unfortunate that there are a few groups that claim to be Muslims, but they believe in a prophet after Prophet Muhammad. These groups cannot be Muslim. The Qur'an confirms that Prophet Muhammad ﷺ is the last and the seal of all Prophets and messengers. Al-Qur'an, too, is the final message from God.

The messengers and Their Books

While all prophets and messengers taught the same message of tawheed, only five were given revelations in the form of a book. These books contained the message of tawheed along with other teachings such as morality, worship, the Day of Judgment, and the belief in Heaven and Hell. The messengers whom we are told received books are Prophet Ibraheem, Prophet Dawood, Prophet Musa, Prophet Isa, and Prophet Muhammad peace be upon all of them. These messengers received special books that had specific names:

A19

Prophet	His Book	
Prophet Ibraheem	Al-Suhuf	صحف إبراهيم
Prophet Musa	At-Tawrah (Torah)	التوراة
Prophet Dawood	Zaboor (Psalms)	الزبور
Prophet Isa	Al-Injeel (Bible)	الإنجيل
Prophet Muhammad	Al-Qur'an	القرآن

As you learned earlier, Prophet Nuh was the first messenger. However, the first messenger who received a written message was Prophet Ibraheem. He was given the first scripture known as the Suhuf, or the scrolls. The Suhuf contained the true message of tawheed along with other teachings of Allah ﷻ. However, many years after he died, people began to corrupt and change the true teachings described in the Suhuf. This caused the people to eventually forget the true message of Allah ﷻ. The need for another written message or a book became urgent. Prophet Musa was chosen to be the next messenger. Allah ﷻ gave him At-Tawrah (the Torah) as a guide for his people. Some time after his death, Prophet Dawood and Prophet Isa were sent as messengers. They too offered to their peoples books of God. As before, their people after them corrupted the original teachings.

The last and seal of all prophets was Muhammad ﷺ. Allah ﷻ provided Prophet Muhammad ﷺ with Al-Qur'an. Al-Qur'an has never changed since its revelation more than 1,400 years ago and it will remain unchanged until the Day of Judgment. It is exactly the same as it was when first revealed by Allah ﷻ. Allah promised in the Qur'an that He will protect His last book against any change or loss.

Allah says:

﴿ إِنَّا نَحْنُ نَزَّلْنَا ٱلذِّكْرَ وَإِنَّا لَهُۥ لَحَٰفِظُونَ ﴾ الحجر: ٩

"We revealed this book and We will surely protect it."
[Surat-ul-Hijr 15:9]

Subhanallah! This is why there was no need for another prophet or messenger after Prophet Muhammad ﷺ.

Chapter Review

Activity Time

Draw a map which shows where at least twenty prophets and messengers delivered their messages.

Think Critically

1. Compare and contrast the characteristics of Allah's prophets and messengers.
2. What are the similarities and differences between prophets and other great Muslim personalities?
3. List all the suwar in the Qur'an that are named after prophets or messengers.

Lesson Review

1. What is the message that all prophets taught to their families and peoples?

2. What are the similarities between prophets and messengers?

3. What is the difference between a prophet and a messenger?

4. How many prophets and messengers are mentioned in the Qur'an altogether? How many were prophets and how many were messengers?

5. Did all messengers receive books from Allah? Explain.

6. Draw a table showing the names of the messengers who received books, and the names of these books.

UNIT A

Tawheed: The Faith of All Prophets

CHAPTER THREE

Word Watch

Tawheed-ul-Khaliq	توحيد الخالق
Tawheed-ul-ebadah	توحيد العبادة
Tawheed-ul-Asmaa'-was-Sifaat	توحيد الأسماء والصفات
Shahadah (testimony of faith)	شَهادة
Kufr	كُفر
Shirk	شِرك

The Meaning of Tawheed

Tawheed is an Arabic word which means believing in and worshipping one God. tawheed is the most important belief in Islam. The English word for tawheed is monotheism.

Surat-ul-Ikhlas is one of the shortest suwar (plural of surah) in Al-Qur'an. But, it is one of the most important. This surah explains the idea of tawheed. tawheed simply means the belief in one God, the true Creator of the universe, and worshipping Him alone.

Allah is "One" without a partner and unique without a match. Allah is the first and the last, and He knows everything. He is the only One worthy of worship, and no one is capable of being God except Him. Believing in tawheed (monotheism) is the most important part of being a Muslim. Do you know that a person cannot become a Muslim without saying the Shahadah?

Words of Wisdom

أَشْهَدُ أَنْ لا إِلهَ إِلا الله وأشهد أنَّ محمداً رسولُ الله

I bear witness there is no god but Allah (God) and that Muhammad is the Messenger of God.

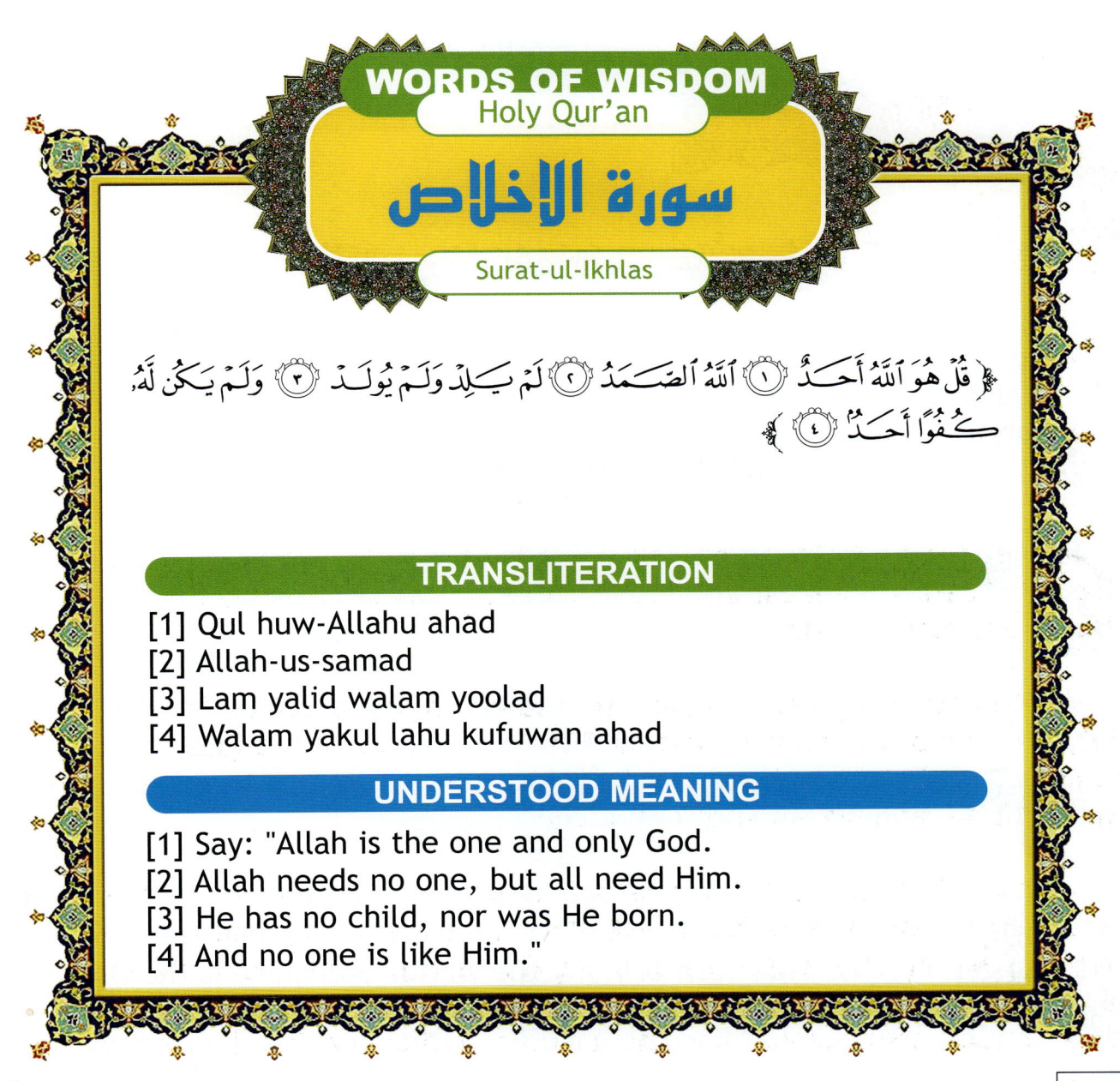

WORDS OF WISDOM
Holy Qur'an

سورة الإخلاص

Surat-ul-Ikhlas

﴿ قُلْ هُوَ ٱللَّهُ أَحَدٌ ۝١ ٱللَّهُ ٱلصَّمَدُ ۝٢ لَمْ يَلِدْ وَلَمْ يُولَدْ ۝٣ وَلَمْ يَكُن لَّهُۥ كُفُوًا أَحَدٌۢ ۝٤ ﴾

TRANSLITERATION

[1] Qul huw-Allahu ahad
[2] Allah-us-samad
[3] Lam yalid walam yoolad
[4] Walam yakul lahu kufuwan ahad

UNDERSTOOD MEANING

[1] Say: "Allah is the one and only God.
[2] Allah needs no one, but all need Him.
[3] He has no child, nor was He born.
[4] And no one is like Him."

Kufr and Shirk

Some people think that there is no god. They claim that the universe somehow just happened without a creator. This is called kufr كفر or disbelief. Others think that there are many gods who helped create this world. This is called shirk شرك (polytheism) and it is the opposite of tawheed (monotheism). Therefore, shirk is the act of believing in or worshipping false gods in addition to our true Creator.

All of these beliefs are rejected in Islam. In fact, to disbelieve in God or to believe in another creator or creators is the worst possible sin. Allah says:

Words of Wisdom

﴿ إِنَّ ٱللَّهَ لَا يَغْفِرُ أَن يُشْرَكَ بِهِۦ وَيَغْفِرُ مَا دُونَ ذَٰلِكَ لِمَن يَشَآءُ وَمَن يُشْرِكْ بِٱللَّهِ فَقَدِ ٱفْتَرَىٰٓ إِثْمًا عَظِيمًا ﴾ النساء: ٤٨

"Allah does not forgive associating partners with Him; but He may forgive anything else, to whom He pleases; to set up partners with Allah is to commit a most heinous sin indeed." [4:48]

The Three Parts of Tawheed

In order to understand the idea of tawheed, scholars in Islam have divided tawheed into three different parts.

1 Tawheed-ul-Khaliq توحيد الخالق : Belief in One Creator

Tawheed-ul-Khaliq, which scholars also call "توحيد الربوبية Tawheed-ur-Ruboobiyyah," is to believe that Allah (God) is the only creator of the world. God alone is the One Who created the universe. As you

▲ *Stone Fish. Yes this is a fish, NOT a stone. Can you see its mouth or eyes?*

learned earlier, one of Allah's names is Al Khaliq, or The Creator.

Tawheed-ul-Khaliq also means that Allah alone provides care to all of His creations. He alone controls the universe and allows things to happen. When something happens, it only happens with Allah's permission.

Tawheed-ul-Khaliq is also called tawheed-ur-Ruboobiyyah which means belief in one lord.

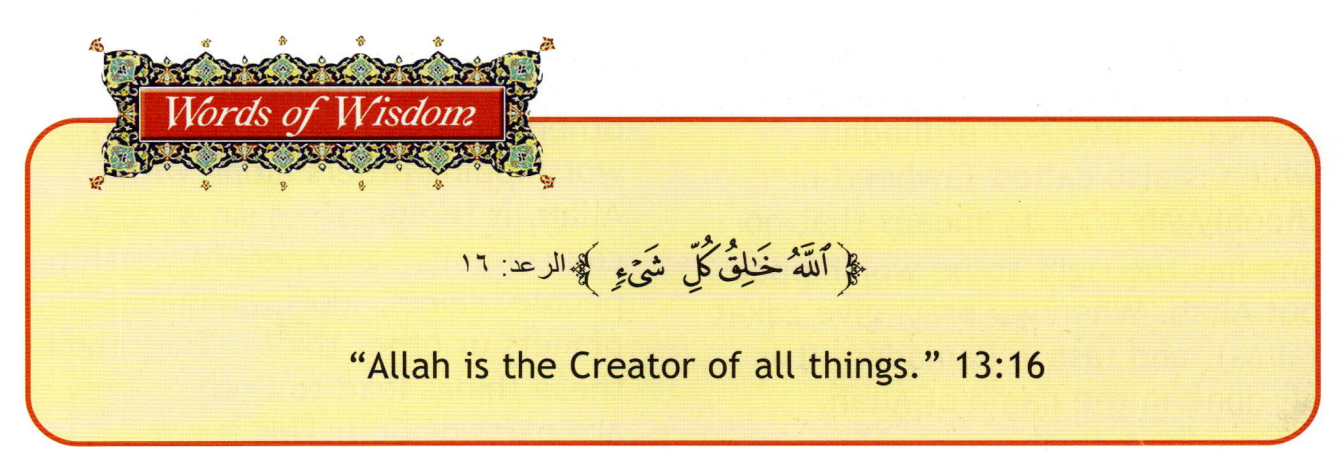

Words of Wisdom

﴿ اَللّٰهُ خَالِقُ كُلِّ شَيْءٍ ﴾ الرعد: ١٦

"Allah is the Creator of all things." 13:16

A25

▲ *Do you know what this beautiful flower is?*

The Prophet Muhammad ﷺ explained the concept of Allah's control over the universe. He said: "If all of mankind gathered together in order to help you, they would only be able to help you as much as Allah had already permitted. Also, if all of mankind gathered together to harm you, they would only be able to harm you as much as Allah had already permitted."

2 Tawheed-ul-Ibadah توحيد العبادة : Worshipping One God

Tawheed-ul-Ibadah توحيد العبادة is one of the most important parts of tawheed. Tawheed-ul-Ibadah, which is also called Tawheed-ul-Uloohiyyah توحيد الألوهية means that no one has the right to be worshipped but Allah. When we pray, give zakat (alms), and fast in Ramadan, it is all done in the name of Allah.

All actions of ibadah should be done for Allah alone. Worshipping others instead of Allah, or even worshipping others along with Allah, is the greatest sin anyone can commit. Many people worship people, saints, idols, animals, planets or other things. They think these things lead to God, or they are parts of God. This is not

▲ *Salah is the act of worshipping the One True God.*

tawheed, and these practices are rejected in Islam.

Ibadah should be done directly to Allah, not through anyone or anything else. For example, many people think that they have to pray or communicate with God through a religious person or a religious leader. When they ask God for forgiveness, they do it through a saint or a religious person. In Islam, you pray, make supplication (du'aa'), and perform all acts of worship to Allah directly. Muslims repent and seek His forgiveness privately. Allah can see and hear you whenever you say or even whisper your prayers, no matter where you are. He is very loving and very close to us.

Words of Wisdom

Holy Qur'an

﴿ قُلْ إِنَّمَا أُمِرْتُ أَنْ أَعْبُدَ ٱللَّهَ وَلَا أُشْرِكَ بِهِۦ إِلَيْهِ أَدْعُوا۟ وَإِلَيْهِ مَتَابِ ﴾ الرعد: ٣٦

Say, "I am commanded to worship Allah alone, and not to join partners with Him. Unto Him do I call, and unto Him is my return." [13:36]

UNIT A CHAPTER 3

Words of Wisdom — Holy Qur'an

﴿ وَقَالَ رَبُّكُمُ ادْعُونِي أَسْتَجِبْ لَكُمْ ﴾ غافر: ٦٠

And your Lord says, "Call on Me; I will answer your (Prayer)." [40:60]

﴿ وَإِذَا سَأَلَكَ عِبَادِي عَنِّي فَإِنِّي قَرِيبٌ أُجِيبُ دَعْوَةَ الدَّاعِ إِذَا دَعَانِ فَلْيَسْتَجِيبُوا لِي وَلْيُؤْمِنُوا بِي لَعَلَّهُمْ يَرْشُدُونَ ﴾ البقرة: ١٨٦

When My servants ask you about Me, I am indeed close (to them): I listen to the prayer of everyone when he calls on Me. Let them also listen to My call, and believe in Me so they may walk in the right way. [2:186]

Words of Wisdom — Ahadeeth Shareefah

قال رسول الله ﷺ:

١- "إذا سألت فاسأل الله وإذا استعنت فاستعن بالله" رواه البخاري عن ابن عباس

٢- "من حلف بغير الله فقد أشرك."

رواه الترمذي عن ابن عمر

The Prophet Muhammad ﷺ said:

1- If you ask (something) in prayer ask only Allah, and if you seek help, seek it only from Allah.   (narrated by Bukhari)
2- Anyone who swears by anything other than God is committing an act of shirk, or disbelief.   (narrated by Tirmithi)

3   Tawheed-ul-Asmaa' was-Sifaat : توحيد الأسماء والصفات

Belief in the high attributes of the One True God

Allah is One, but He has ninety-nine names or attributes that we are made aware of. We understand who our Creator is through His many names. Each attribute has a meaning that is only for God. Tawheed-ul-Asmaa' was-Sifaat means that Allah's names and attributes can only describe Him and no one else. For example, one of Allah's names is Al-Qawiyy, or the Powerful. A human being can also be described as powerful, or qawiyy. We can say that he or she is a powerful fighter, or a strong leader. However, they are not nearly as powerful as Allah. The name of the attribute is perhaps the same, but the meaning and quality of it is extremely different.

Words of Wisdom

Holy Qur'an

﴿ اللَّهُ لَآ إِلَٰهَ إِلَّا هُوَ لَهُ ٱلْأَسْمَآءُ ٱلْحُسْنَىٰ ﴾ طه: ٨

Allah! there is no god but He! To Him belong the Most Beautiful names. [20:8]

A29

UNIT A CHAPTER 3

Benefits of Tawheed

1. It makes us depend on Allah alone and not fear people. Tawheed teaches us that no one can hurt us without the permission of the Creator.

2. It makes people equal since all are created by the same One Creator.

3. It unites humanity since it teaches us believe in the same God, the same message, and perform the same kinds of worship.

4. It frees man from worshipping other humans.

Words of Wisdom

Hadeeth Shareef

عن ابن عباس رضي الله عنهما قال:
كنت خلف رسول الله ﷺ يوما فقال: "يا غلام إني أعلمك كلمات احفظ الله يحفظك احفظ الله تجده تجاهك إذا سألت فاسأل الله وإذا استعنت فاستعن بالله واعلم أن الأمة لو اجتمعت على أن ينفعوك بشيء لم ينفعوك إلا بشيء قد كتبه الله لك ولو اجتمعوا على أن يضروك بشيء لم يضروك إلا بشيء قد كتبه الله عليك رفعت الأقلام وجفت الصحف"
رواه الترمذي وقال هذا حديث حسن صحيح

Abdullah Ibn Abbas narrated: One day I was riding behind rasoolullah ﷺ and he said to me:

Oh son, I am going to teach you a few words, Remember Allah so He will remember you. Remember Allah, so He will support you wherever you are. If you ask for anything, ask Allah [first], and if you seek help, ask the help of Allah [first]. And know that if all the people gather to do good for you, they will not be able to do that unless Allah wants it to happen, and if they gather to hurt you, they will not be able to do that unless Allah wants it to happen. The pens have been lifted the ink on the pages has dried (meaning, Allah has decided this and no one can change it).   Reported in At-Tirmithi

Chapter Review

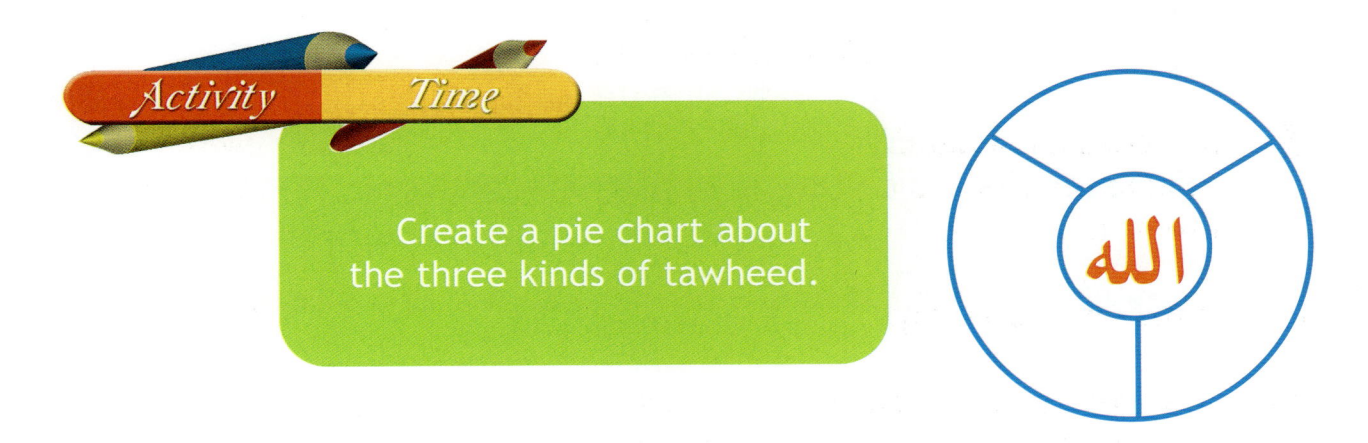

Activity Time

Create a pie chart about the three kinds of tawheed.

Think Critically

Explain the differences among the three kinds of tawheed.

Lesson Review

1. What is the meaning of tawheed?

2. What is the first thing that a person says when he or she becomes a Muslim?

3. Explain Kufr and Shirk.

4. Name and briefly explain the three different parts of tawheed.

5. What are the benefits of believing in tawheed?

UNIT A

Away From Tawheed

CHAPTER FOUR

Pre-reading Questions

1. What is the opposite of tawheed?
2. What does shirk mean?
3. How bad is it to believe in or worship anything other than God?

Word Watch

Shirk (Polytheism)	شِرك
Mushrik	مُشرك
Shirk Al Asghar	الشرك الأصغر
Ar-Riyaa'	الرِّياء
Sihr	سِحر

Introduction

In the lesson about tawheed we learned how Islam stresses the importance of the One and Only God. In this lesson we are going to learn about shirk, which means believing in other Gods along with Allah and worshipping them. **Shirk** is a major sin in Islam and in this lesson we will learn why.

Shirk Explained?

Shirk شرك is the opposite of tawheed. If tawheed is to worship the One and only God, then shirk is to worship something other than Allah. Shirk is the worst sin in Islam. A person who falls into Shirk is called **Mushrik** مُشرك. Allah says in the Qur'an:

﴿ إِنَّ ٱللَّهَ لَا يَغْفِرُ أَن يُشْرَكَ بِهِۦ وَيَغْفِرُ مَا دُونَ ذَٰلِكَ لِمَن يَشَآءُ وَمَن يُشْرِكْ بِٱللَّهِ فَقَدِ ٱفْتَرَىٰٓ إِثْمًا عَظِيمًا ﴾ النساء: ٤٨

"Surely Allah does not forgive that anything should be associated with Him, and forgives what is besides that to whomsoever He pleases; and whoever worships anything with Allah, he indeed commits a great sin." [4:48]

Human beings were created to worship Allah, their only true Creator, Who is also the Creator of the whole universe. Allah ﷻ says in the Qur'an:

﴿ ٱللَّهُ خَٰلِقُ كُلِّ شَىْءٍ وَهُوَ ٱلْوَٰحِدُ ٱلْقَهَّٰرُ ﴾ الرعد: ١٦

"Allah is the Creator of all things, and He is the One, the Supreme." [13:16]

﴿ وَمَا خَلَقْتُ ٱلْجِنَّ وَٱلْإِنسَ إِلَّا لِيَعْبُدُونِ ﴾ الذاريات: ٥٦

"I have not created jinn or mankind except for my worship." [51:56]

By committing shirk a person is going against the statement of tawheed.

لا إله إلا الله

La ilaha illAllah

People become Muslim when they believe in and declare the Shahadah, but they depart from Islam when they act against it. Believing in other gods beside Allah is an act against Shahadah and causes a person to go away from tawheed and out of Islam.

Islam is a religion that teaches pure monotheism. Monotheism means the belief in One God only. Remember how the Arabs during Jahiliyyah used to practice polytheism, which is believing in and worshipping many gods. Both the Qur'an and Sunnah of the Prophet Muhammad ﷺ stress that there is only one God.

UNIT A CHAPTER 4

Some people during ancient times invented false religions which called to worship many idols instead of worshipping Allah, the One and only true Creator of man and the universe.

Types of Shirk

In the tawheed lesson we mentioned 3 different categories of tawheed. In the section that you are about to read we will revisit the three categories of tawheed, but this time we will look at how shirk can be committed by acting against the three different categories of tawheed.

1 Shirk in Ar-Ruboobiyyah   شِرك الرُّبوبية

As Muslims we believe that it is Allah alone Who creates, controls and maintains the universe. The belief that other people or things shared in the act of creating, controlling and or maintaining the universe is a form of shirk. For example, ancient Greeks and Romans used to believe in many gods and goddesses. Their gods had names like Zeus, Athena, Eros and Mercury. In Arabia and elsewhere, they used to worship idols and statues hoping that they would help them get closer to God. In Hinduism, a religion followed in India and other parts of the world, people also believe in

Some idol worshippers made their false gods from gold, but this does not make their false beliefs true.

and worship many gods and goddesses. Each god or goddess has a role to play in creating or controlling parts of this world. AstaghfiruAllah! This is a form of shirk and Islam rejects all shirk.

Many Christians believe that God has three parts:
1. **God the father,**
2. **God the son, or Jesus Christ**
3. **God the Holy Spirit.**

In Christianity this is known as the Trinity. It says that the one God consists of three persons.

As Muslims we know that God is the only Creator of the Universe. God or Allah does not have a father or a son and cannot be divided into two or three persons.

Many of the people who worship idols, people or other things believe in God as the Creator of the world. But they think that God somehow is also part of these things or people that they worship. Others do not believe in one God, but believe in many gods. These imagined gods and goddesses sometimes fight and disagree.

A35

2 Shirk in Ibadah
شِرك في العِبادة

There are a few categories of shirk in ibadah, or worship.

Types of Shirk in Ibadah

Anyone who directs any act of worship to something other than Allah falls into shirk. Worshipping humans, animals, idols or anything else is strictly forbidden in Islam. Actions involving prayer, supplication, bowing and prostration are clear examples of worship. Those who commit this type of shirk have moved away from Islam. However, there are other examples of worshipping other than Allah which can be also described as acts of shirk. Sadly, some Muslims worship saints or travel to graves to ask for help from dead people. They make tawaaf around these graves and they sacrifice in the name of the dead people. All of these are major forms of shirk and must be avoided. We must offer our worship only to Allah, not to anyone or anything else.

In the Qur'an, Allah says

﴿ قُلْ إِنَّ صَلَاتِي وَنُسُكِي وَمَحْيَايَ وَمَمَاتِي لِلَّهِ رَبِّ الْعَالَمِينَ ﴾

"Say, 'Truly, my prayer, my sacrifice, my life and my death are all for Allah, Lord of the worlds'." [6:162]

As you learned earlier, shirk will not be forgiven and whoever dies while committing it will not be able to enter Jannah. But remember, Allah is Al Ghafoor, which means the Most Forgiving. Allah will accept the repentance of those who repent before they die and they will inshaAllah, be forgiven.

Ash-Shirk-ul-Asghar

الشِّرْكُ الأَصْغَر

(The Minor Shirk)

There are other types of shirk in worship and they are described as **Ash-Shirk-ul-Asghar**. Although these acts do not necessarily automatically take the person beyond the path of Islam, they are still very serious sins.

Mahmood Ibn Lubayd reported that Prophet Muhammad ﷺ said:

"The thing that I fear for you the most is minor shirk." The companions asked "O Messenger of Allah what is minor shirk?" He replied, "Showing off (Ar- Riyaa'), for Allah will say on the Day of

Judgment when people are receiving their rewards, 'Go to those whom you were showing off to in the world and see if you can get any reward from them.'"

Ar-Riyaa' is having insincere intentions and performing acts of worship in order to show off to other people. A person is committing riyaa' if he/she prays in front of people just so the people can think that he or she is a very good Muslim. It is very important for a person to make sure that he/she has pure intentions to only please Allah and nobody else.

Healthy Habit

Always purify your intention when you perform good deeds. Avoid riyaa' or it will wipe out your rewards.

Other forms of minor shirk involve:

▶ **Swearing by other than Allah.** Once, Abdullah Ibn Omar عنه رضي الله saw a man swearing by his father, and another swearing by Al-Ka'bah, so he told them not to do that. Then he said: "I heard Prophet Muhammad ﷺ once saying:

"مَنْ حَلَفَ بِغَيرِ اللهِ فَقَدْ أَشْرَكَ"

'Whoever swears by other than Allah has committed an act of shirk.'"

Here, rasoolullah means minor shirk.

▶ **Following one's desires while not obeying Allah and His Prophet.** Some people love money,

A37

games, fame and other worldly things more than they love Allah. They will do forbidden things to have more fun. They do such things even if they have to disobey Allah and displease Him. Some people even skip prayers in order to keep playing video games or watch TV. To them, their desires are more important than Allah ﷺ. Allah says in the Qur'an,

﴿ أَفَرَءَيْتَ مَنِ ٱتَّخَذَ إِلَٰهَهُۥ هَوَىٰهُ وَأَضَلَّهُ ٱللَّهُ عَلَىٰ عِلْمٍ ﴾

"Have you then seen the one who follows his low desire as god, and Allah has made him go astray although he has knowledge?" [45:23]

Healthy Habit

Always obey Allah first, and avoid disobeying Him for a little fun in this life.

▶ **Wearing charms or using spells to weaken jinn or evil spirits.** Some people wear certain charms and use spells to protect themselves or children from jinn. They think that these things have the power to protect them from the harm of devils. These people are committing minor acts of shirk. Instead, they should pray, read Qur'an, or make dua'a to Allah, asking Him for His protection. This is what rasoolullah used to do when he wanted Allah's protection against evil powers.

▶ **To believe in fortune telling and fortune tellers.** Prophet Muhammad ﷺ once said,

من أتى كاهناً فصدّقه بما يقول فقد كفر بما أنزلَ على محمد ﷺ.

رواه أبو داود

"Whoever visits a fortune teller and believes in what he says, he has disbelieved in what has been revealed to Muhammad," Reported by Imam Abu Dawood.

Reading horoscopes, for example, is a type of fortune telling. Muslims must avoid reading them and believing them.

****

It is important to understand that just because these forms of shirk are called minor shirk, it does not mean that they are not serious. The reason they are called minor shirk is because they are not as obvious as compared to major shirk. Sometimes it is hard for a person to know they are committing Ash-Shirk-ul-Asghar. So, we should be very careful not to commit **Ash-Shirk-ul-Asghar**.

3 Shirk in Al-Asmaa' was-Sifaat — شِرك في الأسماء والصفات

You learned earlier that Allah has the greatest names and attributes. They are also called Al-Asmaa'-ul-Husna. Therefore, you know that God is unique and none is like Him. However, many people fall into shirk because they do not believe in the names and attributes of God properly. They may give God some names or attributes that are unfitting to Allah ﷻ. Here are examples of shirk in Al-Asmaa' and As-Sifaat.

▶ **An-Nafi:** Denying the great attributes of Allah. Some people deny that Allah has the greatest qualities and attributes. They say the names of God like Ar-Rahman, Al-Kareem, or Al-Qawiyy have no actual meaning. They claim that God is not merciful or generous or powerful, and that these are just empty names. This is the worst type of shirk in Al-Asmaa' and As-Sifaat. Allah has the best names

A39

and attributes and He is so great because these attributes are real and actual.

▶ **At-Tashbeeh:** Giving Allah ungodly attributes. Some people give God human qualities, like getting sick, tired, jealous or greedy. Astaghfirullah! For example, some religious books say that God created the world in six days, got tired then He rested on the seventh day. This is very wrong. God is like no other and that means we cannot compare Him to humans or to any of His creations.

▶ **At-Tahreef:** Changing the meaning of God's attributes. Some people understand the meaning of God's names or attributes in an incorrect manner. We should always understand the meaning of Allah's names and attributes the way God or the Prophet explain then. For example, some would say that God's name Al-Wadood does not mean the loving, because that makes God emotional like people or animals. Therefore, when Allah describes Himself in the Qur'an as loving this thing or that, they say it means that Allah wants it. That is also wrong. Allah loves people and His good creation, but the quality of His love is greater and different than that of people or animals.

Effects of Shirk

1 Shirk puts humans in a very low status.

Allah created jinns, animals, humans, and many other things. But Allah says that man is created in the highest of forms. This means that human beings are put above all other creations. Humans are known as Khaleefat-ullah fil-Ardh (the vicegerents of Allah on Earth). When a person commits shirk, then he falls from a very high status to the lowest one.

Allah says:

﴿وَمَن يُشْرِكْ بِاللَّهِ فَكَأَنَّمَا خَرَّ مِنَ السَّمَاءِ فَتَخْطَفُهُ الطَّيْرُ أَوْ تَهْوِي بِهِ الرِّيحُ فِي مَكَانٍ سَحِيقٍ﴾

"Whoever claims partners unto Allah, it is as if he had fallen from the sky and the birds had snatched him or the wind had blown him to a very low place." [Surat-ul-Hajj 22:31]

2. Shirk is the cause of evil and superstitions.

It is because of shirk that many people believe in the powers of jinn and spirits. Some people think fortune tellers can predict the future or cause something to happen or not to happen. They do that because they don't have proper faith and tawheed in their hearts. All these are forms of evil practices that lead to shirk.

Abu Hurayrah رضي الله عنه narrated that rasoolullah ﷺ said:

" اجْتَنِبوا الموبقات: الشِّرْكُ بالله والسِّحْرْ "

رواه البخاري

"Avoid the destructive sins; shirk and witchcraft."

Reported in Al-Bukhari

3. Committing shirk is injustice.

Injustice means to deny someone's right or to treat someone unfairly. By worshipping and praising something instead of Allah, we are being ungrateful and unjust to Allah. Only Allah has the right to be worshipped.

﴿ وَإِذْ قَالَ لُقْمَٰنُ لِٱبْنِهِۦ وَهُوَ يَعِظُهُۥ يَٰبُنَىَّ لَا تُشْرِكْ بِٱللَّهِ إِنَّ ٱلشِّرْكَ لَظُلْمٌ عَظِيمٌ ﴾

"Luqman said to his son while advising him, 'Oh my son! Do not call partners to Allah. Indeed shirk is a great injustice.'"
[Luqman 31: 13]

4. Shirk causes anxiety and fear.

A person who commits shirk lives in constant fear and anxiety. He fears powers like this idol, or that fire, or that spirit etc. While trying to make one idol happy, he is afraid another one will be angry with him. Remember that we should only fear Allah.

A41

UNIT A CHAPTER 4

Idols that used to be worshipped by disbelievers in Arabia and around the world

5. Shirk wipes off rewards in the Hereafter.

Heaven is forbidden to those who associate partners with Allah. No person who commits shirk will be allowed to enter Paradise. Also, Allah does not accept the good deeds of a mushrik. Therefore, those who commit shirk will have no rewards for whatever good deeds they do in this life. Allah will reward them during this life only by giving them more wealth, health and entertainment. But they will not win any rewards in the next life and they will never win Jannah. This is because they disbelieve in Allah or worship others with Him. Allah describes this in the Qur'an:

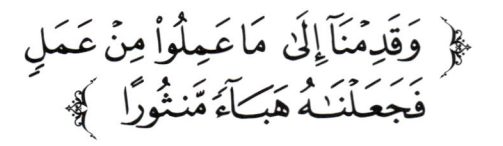

$$\text{وَقَدِمْنَآ إِلَىٰ مَا عَمِلُوا۟ مِنْ عَمَلٍ فَجَعَلْنَـٰهُ هَبَآءً مَّنثُورًا}$$

"And We will come to what deeds they have done, so We shall make them as scattered floating dust." [25:23]

Activity Time

Create a table for the shirk against the three types of tawheed. List three examples of shirk under each type. Use the example below to create your table.

	Tawheed-ur-Ruboobiyyah	Tawheed-ul-Ibadah	Tawheed-ul-Asmaa'
1.			
2.			
3.			

A43

STORY TIME

The People of Prophet Musa

The people of Prophet Musa had to leave their homes in Egypt to escape the evil Pharaoh. While searching for a new home, Musa's people wandered in the desert of Sinai for many years. One day, Musa عليه السّلام received Allah's order to climb a high mountain there. Prophet Musa عليه السّلام had to stay there for forty days and nights praying to Allah and listening to what Allah would tell him and his people. But forty days and nights seemed a very long time. And while Musa عليه السّلام was away, his people became impatient. They decided to make a calf out of gold and worship it. When Musa عليه السّلام came down from the mountain, he saw the calf and became very angry. He smashed the calf into pieces and scolded his people so much that they felt ashamed of themselves. "You must never, ever worship anything else apart from Allah," Musa عليه السّلام instructed them.

Musa عليه السّلام had brought a book to his people which Allah had revealed to him on the mountain. This book is called At-Tawrah, or the Torah. In At-Tawrah, it is stated that men should never worship anything else except Allah. They must never kill a fellow man. They must not take things which do not belong to them. They must be good to their parents and to one another.

Prophet Musa's people understood then that they had been very ungrateful to Allah. It was Allah Who had created them and saved them from Pharaoh and his soldiers. They prayed to Allah and thanked Him for what He had done for them. They asked for His forgiveness and made a promise that they would do good deeds.

Allah سُبْحانه وتعالى forgave those who were ashamed of the bad deeds they had done and wanted to return to Allah.

Chapter Review

Think Critically

1. Why is shirk the worst sin man can ever commit?

2. Why do you think Allah would not accept the good deeds of a person if he or she is a mushrik?

Lesson Review

1. What is shirk?

2. Describe how one can commit shirk in tawheed-ur-Ruboobiyyah?

3. Describe how one can commit shirk in tawheed-ul-Ibadah?

4. Describe how one can commit shirk in tawheed-ul-Asmaa' Wassifaat?

5. Does Allah forgive shirk? Support your answer with an ayah from the Holy Qur'an.

6. Is Ash-Shirk-ul-Asghar not very important?

7. What are the five effects of committing shirk?

8. How did the people of Musa عليه السّلام commit shirk?

UNIT A CHAPTER 5
LESSON ONE

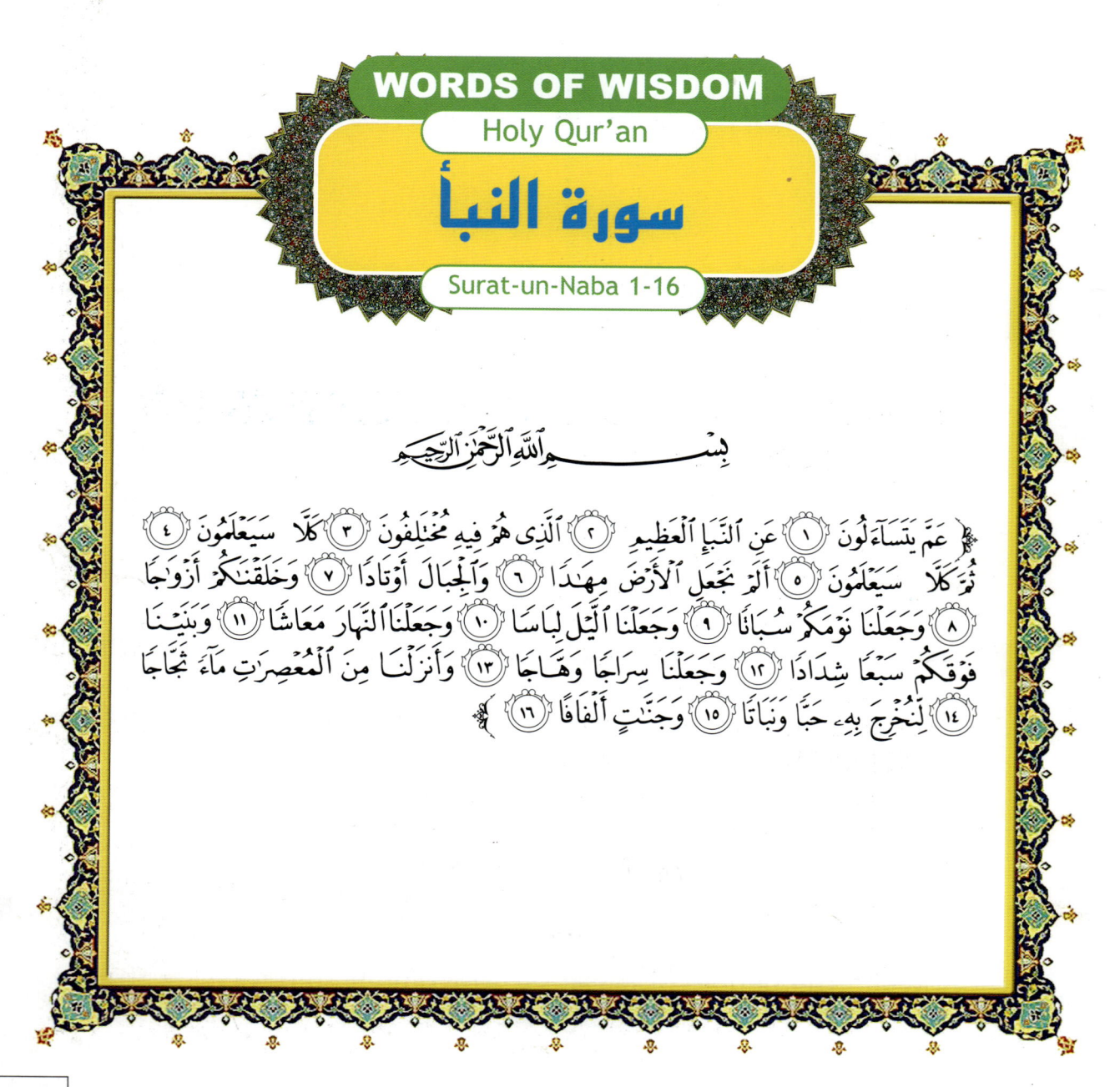

Surat-un-Naba': 1

WORDS OF WISDOM
Holy Qur'an

سورة النبأ

Surat-un-Naba 1-16

بِسْمِ ٱللَّهِ ٱلرَّحْمَٰنِ ٱلرَّحِيمِ

عَمَّ يَتَسَاءَلُونَ ﴿١﴾ عَنِ ٱلنَّبَإِ ٱلْعَظِيمِ ﴿٢﴾ ٱلَّذِى هُمْ فِيهِ مُخْتَلِفُونَ ﴿٣﴾ كَلَّا سَيَعْلَمُونَ ﴿٤﴾ ثُمَّ كَلَّا سَيَعْلَمُونَ ﴿٥﴾ أَلَمْ نَجْعَلِ ٱلْأَرْضَ مِهَٰدًا ﴿٦﴾ وَٱلْجِبَالَ أَوْتَادًا ﴿٧﴾ وَخَلَقْنَٰكُمْ أَزْوَٰجًا ﴿٨﴾ وَجَعَلْنَا نَوْمَكُمْ سُبَاتًا ﴿٩﴾ وَجَعَلْنَا ٱلَّيْلَ لِبَاسًا ﴿١٠﴾ وَجَعَلْنَا ٱلنَّهَارَ مَعَاشًا ﴿١١﴾ وَبَنَيْنَا فَوْقَكُمْ سَبْعًا شِدَادًا ﴿١٢﴾ وَجَعَلْنَا سِرَاجًا وَهَّاجًا ﴿١٣﴾ وَأَنزَلْنَا مِنَ ٱلْمُعْصِرَٰتِ مَاءً ثَجَّاجًا ﴿١٤﴾ لِّنُخْرِجَ بِهِۦ حَبًّا وَنَبَاتًا ﴿١٥﴾ وَجَنَّٰتٍ أَلْفَافًا ﴿١٦﴾

TRANSLITERATION

1. Amma yatasa'aloon
2. An-in-naba-il 'athee
3. Allathee hum feehi mukhtalifoon
4. Kalla saya'lamoon
5. Thumma kalla saya'lamoon
6. Alam naj'al-il-arda mihada
7. Waljibala awtada
8. Wakhalaqnakum azwaja
9. Waja'alna nawmakum subata
10. Waja'alnal-layla libasa
11. Waja'alna-nnahara ma'asha
12. Wabanayna fawqakum sab'an shidada
13. Waja'alna sirajaw-wahhaja
14. Wa-anzalna min-al-mu'sirati ma'an thajjaja
15. Linukhrija bihi habbaw-wanabata
16. Wajannatin alfafa

UNDERSTOOD MEANING

[78:1] About what do they ask one another?
[78:2] About the great event,
[78:3] About which they disagree
[78:4] Nay! they shall soon come to know
[78:5] Nay! Nay! they shall soon know.
[78:6] Didn't We make the Earth a landscape?
[78:7] And made the mountains as pegs?
[78:8] And We created you in pairs,
[78:9] And We made your sleep to be rest (to you),
[78:10] And We made the night to be a covering,
[78:11] And We made the day for seeking livelihood
[78:12] And We made above you seven strong [heavens],
[78:13] And We made [the sun as] a shining lamp
[78:14] And We send down from the clouds water pouring heavily,
[78:15] So that We bring forth seeds and plants,
[78:16] And lush gardens dense and luxuriant.

UNIT A
CHAPTER 5
LESSON TWO

Surat-un-Naba': 2

WORDS OF WISDOM
Holy Qur'an

سورة النبأ

Surat-un-Naba 17-30

بِسْمِ ٱللَّهِ ٱلرَّحْمَٰنِ ٱلرَّحِيمِ

﴿ إِنَّ يَوْمَ ٱلْفَصْلِ كَانَ مِيقَٰتًا ۝ يَوْمَ يُنفَخُ فِى ٱلصُّورِ فَتَأْتُونَ أَفْوَاجًا ۝ وَفُتِحَتِ ٱلسَّمَآءُ فَكَانَتْ أَبْوَٰبًا ۝ وَسُيِّرَتِ ٱلْجِبَالُ فَكَانَتْ سَرَابًا ۝ إِنَّ جَهَنَّمَ كَانَتْ مِرْصَادًا ۝ لِّلطَّٰغِينَ مَـَٔابًا ۝ لَّٰبِثِينَ فِيهَآ أَحْقَابًا ۝ لَّا يَذُوقُونَ فِيهَا بَرْدًا وَلَا شَرَابًا ۝ إِلَّا حَمِيمًا وَغَسَّاقًا ۝ جَزَآءً وِفَاقًا ۝ إِنَّهُمْ كَانُوا۟ لَا يَرْجُونَ حِسَابًا ۝ وَكَذَّبُوا۟ بِـَٔايَٰتِنَا كِذَّابًا ۝ وَكُلَّ شَىْءٍ أَحْصَيْنَٰهُ كِتَٰبًا ۝ فَذُوقُوا۟ فَلَن نَّزِيدَكُمْ إِلَّا عَذَابًا ۝ ﴾

A48

TRANSLITERATION

17. Inna yawm-al-fasli kana meeqata
18. Yawma yunfakhu fissoori fata'toona afwaja
19. Wafutihat-is-sama'o fakanat abwaba
20. Wasuyyirat-iljibalu fakanat saraba
21. Inna jahannama kanat mirsada
22. Littagheena ma'aba
23. Labitheena feeha ahqaba
24. La yathooqoona feeha bardaw-wala sharaba
25. Illa hameemaw-waghassaqa
26. Jazaaw-wifaqa
27. Innahum kanoo la yarjoona hisaba
28. Wakaththaboo bi-ayatina kiththaba
29. Wakulla shay-in ahsaynahu kitaba
30. Fathooqoo falan-nazeedakum illa 'athaba

UNDERSTOOD MEANING

[78:17] Surely the Day of Judgment has a fixed time:
[78:18] That day on which the trumpet shall be blown so you shall come in large groups,
[78:19] And the heaven shall be opened and it shall have gates,
[78:20] And the mountains shall be moved and turn as a mirage
[78:21] Surely hell is in wait,
[78:22] For the evil people, it is their home
[78:23] Living therein for ages.
[78:24] They shall not taste therein cool nor drink
[78:25] But boiling and extremely cold fluids,
[78:26] A penalty that fits their deeds
[78:27] Surely, they didn't expect to be questioned,
[78:28] And they disbelieved in our verses.
[78:29] And We have recorded everything in a book,
[78:30] So taste! for We will give nothing more except punishment

UNIT A CHAPTER 5
LESSON THREE

Surat-un-Naba': 3

WORDS OF WISDOM
Holy Qur'an

سورة النبأ

Surat-un-Naba 31-40

بِسْمِ ٱللَّهِ ٱلرَّحْمَٰنِ ٱلرَّحِيمِ

إِنَّ لِلْمُتَّقِينَ مَفَازًا ۝ حَدَائِقَ وَأَعْنَابًا ۝ وَكَوَاعِبَ أَتْرَابًا ۝ وَكَأْسًا دِهَاقًا ۝ لَا يَسْمَعُونَ فِيهَا لَغْوًا وَلَا كِذَّابًا ۝ جَزَاءً مِّن رَّبِّكَ عَطَاءً حِسَابًا ۝ رَّبِّ ٱلسَّمَٰوَٰتِ وَٱلْأَرْضِ وَمَا بَيْنَهُمَا ٱلرَّحْمَٰنِ لَا يَمْلِكُونَ مِنْهُ خِطَابًا ۝ يَوْمَ يَقُومُ ٱلرُّوحُ وَٱلْمَلَٰٓئِكَةُ صَفًّا لَّا يَتَكَلَّمُونَ إِلَّا مَنْ أَذِنَ لَهُ ٱلرَّحْمَٰنُ وَقَالَ صَوَابًا ۝ ذَٰلِكَ ٱلْيَوْمُ ٱلْحَقُّ فَمَن شَاءَ ٱتَّخَذَ إِلَىٰ رَبِّهِ مَـَٔابًا ۝ إِنَّا أَنذَرْنَٰكُمْ عَذَابًا قَرِيبًا يَوْمَ يَنظُرُ ٱلْمَرْءُ مَا قَدَّمَتْ يَدَاهُ وَيَقُولُ ٱلْكَافِرُ يَٰلَيْتَنِى كُنتُ تُرَٰبًۢا ۝

TRANSLITERATION

31. Inna lilmuttaqeena mafaza
32. Hada-iqa wa'aa'naba
33. Wakawa'iba atraba
34. Waka'san dihaqa
35. La yasma'oona feeha laghwaw-wala kiththaba
36. Jaza'an mir-rabbika 'ata'an hisaba
37. Rabb-is-samawati wal-ardi wama baynahuma-rrahmani la yamlikoona minhu khitaba
38. Yawma yaqoom-ur-roohu walmala-ikatu saffal la yatakallam-oona illa man athina lah-ur-rahmanu waqala sawaba
39. Thalik-al-yawm-ul-haqqu faman sha'a-ttakhatha ila rabbihi ma'aba
40. Inna antharnakum 'athaban qareebay-yawma yanthur-ul-mar'o ma qaddamat yadahu wayaqool-ul-kafiru ya laytanee kuntu turaba

UNDERSTOOD MEANING

[78:31] Surely, the pious will win,
[78:32] Gardens and vineyards,
[78:33] and women of equal age;
[78:34] And a pure cup.
[78:35] They shall not hear therein any vain words or lying.
[78:36] A reward from your Lord, a gift for their deeds:
[78:37] The Lord of the heavens and the Earth and what is between them, the Most Merciful, they shall not be able to talk to Him.
[78:38] The day on which the spirit and the angels shall stand in line; they shall not speak except those whom Allah permits and who speaks the right thing.
[78:39] That is the day of truth, so whoever wants may take the protection of his Lord.
[78:40] Surely We have warned you of a near punishment: the day when man shall see what he did before, and the unbeliever shall say: Oh! I wish I was dust!

A51

3 نوح	2 إِدريس	1 آدم
6 ابراهيم	5 صالح	4 هود
9 اسحاق	8 إِسماعيل	7 لوط
12 ايوب	11 يوسف	10 يعقوب
15 موسى	14 شعيب	13 ذو الكفل
18 سليمان	17 داوود	16 هارون
21 يونس	20 اليسع	19 الياس
24 عيسى	23 يحيى	22 زكريا
	25 محمد	

UNIT B

MANY PROPHETS, ONE GOD

CHAPTER 1	Prophet Hud	**B2**
CHAPTER 2	Prophet Salih	**B12**
CHAPTER 3	Prophet Lut and the People of Sodom	**B22**
CHAPTER 4	Turning to Allah: The Story Of Prophet Younus	**B34**

UNIT B

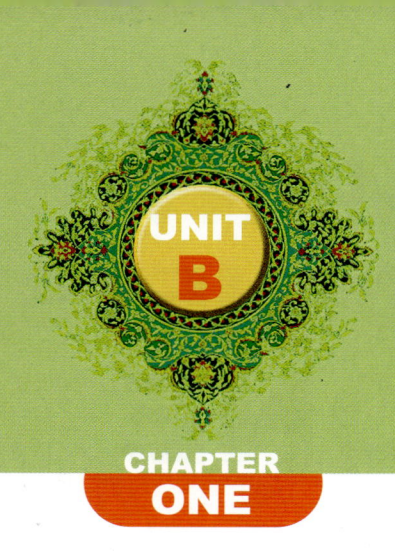

CHAPTER ONE

Prophet Hud عليه السلام

Pre-reading Questions

1. Who were the people of 'Aad?
2. What did the people of 'Aad Worship?
3. Whom did Allah choose as a prophet for 'Aad?
4. How did the people of 'Aad reject Prophet Hud?
5. How did Allah punish the disbelievers among the people of 'Aad?

Word Watch

Hud	هود
Aad	عاد
Iram	إرم
Ubar	أبَر

The People of 'Aad

Many years after Prophet Nuh عليه السلام, there lived a very industrious, hardworking people. They were the people of 'Aad عاد.

'Aad was a King and he was also the grandson of Prophet Nuh. This is why his people and offspring were called the people of 'Aad. The people of 'Aad lived in an ancient city called إرم Iram, a place in the south of present day Saudia Arabia near the borders of

Yemen and Oman. Allah blessed them with great wealth and they lived life in peace and comfort. Allah ﷻ gave them many blessings and made them very successful traders. They were very strong physically and there was no disease in their society. The people of 'Aad built large and beautiful houses. On every hill they built a tower, and they were very proud of their beautiful buildings.

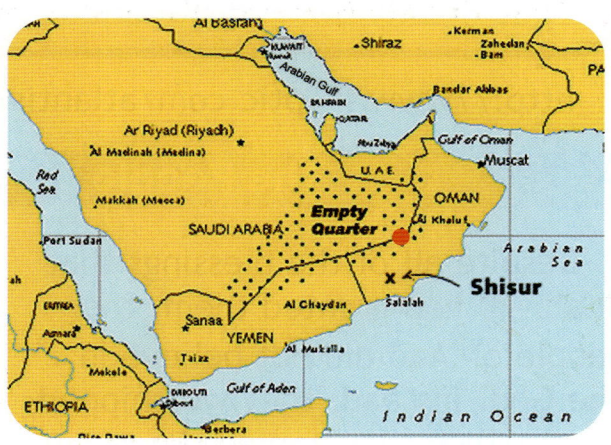

| **Allah** | is المغني Al-Mughni; The Giver of Wealth. |

All money or wealth people have is from Allah.

﴿وَأَنَّهُ هُوَ أَغْنَىٰ وَأَقْنَىٰ ٤٨﴾

"And He is the One who gives wealth and belongings." [53:48]

UNIT B CHAPTER 1

The Ancient City of Ubar

UBAR-A wealthy incense trading post was said to be lost beneath the desert sands of Saudi Arabia. The Koran-the holy book of the Muslims-said the people of Ubar were destroyed because they became corrupted by power and wealth. The city was said to have been swallowed up by the ground. With the help of the space shuttle radar, ruins matching the story of Ubar were found-an incense trading city that had collapsed into a giant sinkhole. While no one can say for sure if the ruins actually were Ubar (no inscription with the actual name of Ubar was found), there is a good chance the site inspired at least some parts of the Ubar stories.

http://www.skeptic.com/atlantis/atlantis3.html

The People of 'Aad Worship Idols

Despite all of the blessings that Allah ﷻ had granted them, the people of 'Aad did not believe in one God. Instead, they worshipped idols, which they carved out of stones. When anything good happened to them, they thanked their idols. Whenever they were in trouble, they prayed to those idols for help. Those people had forgotten all about Prophet Nuh and his message of worshipping one God, or tawheed. They forgot the awful punishment of Allah for worshipping false gods.

Allah Chooses Hud to be a Prophet

Among the people of 'Aad lived a man named Hud. Allah ﷻ chose him as His next prophet. He was from the tribe of 'Aad itself, and was respected because of his noble family and his good manners. He was the great-grandson of Prophet Nuh عليه السلام. Hud was a very patient and kind man. When he received the command of Allah to teach His message, he immedi-

B4

ately did so. He came to the people and said:

"O Brothers, why do you worship stones that you have carved yourself? The idols can not give you anything or take anything away from you. Allah has sent me to you."

Prophet Hud عليه السلام also said to his people:

"Allah has taught you all that you are able to do. He has also given you children and many animals. Therefore you should stop worshipping your false gods. Worship only Allah and obey His commands. Do well and do not commit wrongs and evil. Your Lord is only one, and He alone should be worshipped. He has created you, given you health and wealth, and made you a powerful nation."

Prophet Hud explained to them that the idols would only take them further away from God.

The Holy Qur'an says in Surat Hud:

وَإِلَىٰ عَادٍ أَخَاهُمْ هُودًا قَالَ يَـٰقَوْمِ ٱعْبُدُوا۟ ٱللَّهَ مَا لَكُم مِّنْ إِلَـٰهٍ غَيْرُهُۥٓ إِنْ أَنتُمْ إِلَّا مُفْتَرُونَ ۝

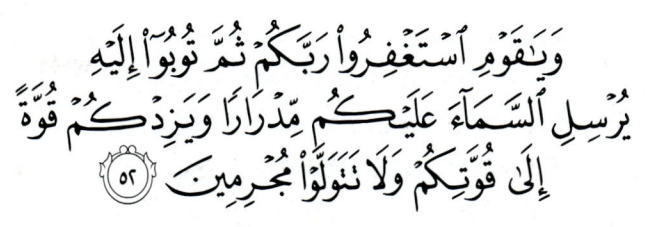

يَـٰقَوْمِ لَآ أَسْـَٔلُكُمْ عَلَيْهِ أَجْرًا إِنْ أَجْرِىَ إِلَّا عَلَى ٱلَّذِى فَطَرَنِىٓ أَفَلَا تَعْقِلُونَ ۝

وَيَـٰقَوْمِ ٱسْتَغْفِرُوا۟ رَبَّكُمْ ثُمَّ تُوبُوٓا۟ إِلَيْهِ يُرْسِلِ ٱلسَّمَآءَ عَلَيْكُم مِّدْرَارًا وَيَزِدْكُمْ قُوَّةً إِلَىٰ قُوَّتِكُمْ وَلَا تَتَوَلَّوْا۟ مُجْرِمِينَ ۝

"And to the people of 'Aad, We sent their brother Hud. He said, "O my people! Worship Allah! You have no other Ilah (god) but Him, certainly, you do nothing but invent (lies)!" [11:50]

"O my people I ask of you no reward for this [Message]. My reward is only from Him Who created me (Allah). Won't you then understand?" [11:51]

"And O my people! Ask forgiveness of your Lord and then repent to Him. He will send you (from the sky) abundant rain, and add strength to your strength, so do not turn away as sinners." [11:52]

The People of 'Aad Reject Prophet Hud

Prophet Hud عليه السلام tried to explain to his people how everything they had was a blessing from Allah. How Allah ﷻ had made them Prophet Nuh's successors, and how He had given them strength and power. The people of 'Aad rejected Prophet Hud's message and continued ridiculing him.

They said:
"We are not going to listen to you. We are not going to let our gods down, just because you tell us so. Who are you, anyway? You are nothing but a liar. If you are not a liar, then prove it."

Allah ﷻ repeated their words in the Qur'an:

﴿ قَالُواْ يَـٰهُودُ مَا جِئْتَنَا بِبَيِّنَةٍ وَمَا نَحْنُ بِتَارِكِىٓ ءَالِهَتِنَا عَن قَوْلِكَ وَمَا نَحْنُ لَكَ بِمُؤْمِنِينَ ﴾

﴿ إِن نَّقُولُ إِلَّا ٱعْتَرَىٰكَ بَعْضُ ءَالِهَتِنَا بِسُوٓءٍ ﴾

"O Hud! No evidence have you brought us, and we shall not leave our gods at your command! And we don't believe in you.
All that we say is that some of our gods have touched you with madness." [Surat Hud 11: 53-54]

Prophet Hud was very sad and disappointed when he heard this. He said to them, "Do you think the houses you have built will last forever? Remember that it is Allah Who has given you your fortunes."

Allah ﷻ recounts in the Qur'an:

﴿ قَالَ إِنِّىٓ أُشْهِدُ ٱللَّهَ وَٱشْهَدُوٓاْ أَنِّى بَرِىٓءٌ مِّمَّا تُشْرِكُونَ ﴾

▲ *The city of Iram, which is now known as Ubar was buried under the sands of the Empty Quarters for thousands of years. Scientists discovered the buried city in 1996 on the border between Saudi Arabia and Oman.*

He (Prophet Hud) said: "I call Allah to witness and bear you witness that I am innocent of your sin. You worship others with Him (Allah)."

﴿ مِن دُونِهِۦ فَكِيدُونِى جَمِيعًا ثُمَّ لَا تُنظِرُونِ ﴾

﴿ إِنِّى تَوَكَّلْتُ عَلَى ٱللَّهِ رَبِّى وَرَبِّكُم مَّا مِن دَآبَّةٍ إِلَّا هُوَ ءَاخِذٌۢ بِنَاصِيَتِهَآ إِنَّ رَبِّى عَلَىٰ صِرَٰطٍ مُّسْتَقِيمٍ ﴾

"So plot against me, all of you, and give me no breaks; I put my trust in Allah. He is my Lord and your Lord!" [11:55]

Despite Prophet Hud's warnings, the people of 'Aad went on worshipping their false gods. He was very disappointed. When he warned the people of 'Aad about the punishment of Allah, they challenged Prophet Hud. They said:

"We don't care. Tell your Lord to send us His punishment."

The Qur'an quotes them as saying:

﴿ قَالُوٓا۟ أَجِئْتَنَا لِنَعْبُدَ ٱللَّهَ وَحْدَهُۥ وَنَذَرَ مَا كَانَ يَعْبُدُ ءَابَآؤُنَا فَأْتِنَا بِمَا تَعِدُنَآ إِن كُنتَ مِنَ ٱلصَّـٰدِقِينَ ﴾

"Then bring down [the punishment] on us that you have threatened, if you are truthful." [7:70]

Allah Punishes the Disbelievers

Shortly afterwards, a huge black cloud appeared in the sky, over the people of 'Aad. When the unbelievers of 'Aad saw it, they said: "This cloud is surely going to bring us some refreshing rain."

But they were very much mistaken. Allah says in the Qur'an:

﴿ فَلَمَّا رَأَوْهُ عَارِضًا مُّسْتَقْبِلَ أَوْدِيَتِهِمْ قَالُوا۟ هَـٰذَا عَارِضٌ مُّمْطِرُنَا ۚ بَلْ هُوَ مَا ٱسْتَعْجَلْتُم بِهِۦ ۖ رِيحٌ فِيهَا عَذَابٌ أَلِيمٌ ﴾

﴿ تُدَمِّرُ كُلَّ شَىْءٍۭ بِأَمْرِ رَبِّهَا فَأَصْبَحُوا۟ لَا يُرَىٰٓ إِلَّا مَسَـٰكِنُهُمْ ۚ كَذَٰلِكَ نَجْزِى ٱلْقَوْمَ ٱلْمُجْرِمِينَ ﴾

"Then when they saw it as a dense cloud coming towards their valleys, they said: 'This is a cloud bringing us rain!' Nay but it is that punishment which you were asking for! A wind wherein is a painful punishment! Destroying everything by the command of its Lord!" [46:24-25]

The clouds grew larger and larger as the wind howled louder and louder. At the first sign of the storm, Prophet Hud had gathered his followers and family and taken them to a safe place. The wind was full of dust and sand. It blew violently for eight continuous days. The people ran into their big houses and beautiful castles to hide. But nothing could save them from the punishment of Allah.

The wind swept everything away. That violent storm did not stop until the entire region was reduced to ruin. The unbelievers were destroyed and swallowed by the sands of the desert. Nothing was left except a few large stones, which were the remains of the houses and towers. Only Prophet Hud عليه السلام and his followers remained unharmed because they believed in Allah and obeyed Him.

UNIT B CHAPTER 1

WORDS OF WISDOM
Holy Qur'an

سورة القمر

Surat-ul-Qamar 18-22

بِسْمِ اللَّهِ الرَّحْمَٰنِ الرَّحِيمِ

كَذَّبَتْ عَادٌ فَكَيْفَ كَانَ عَذَابِي وَنُذُرِ ﴿١٨﴾ إِنَّا أَرْسَلْنَا عَلَيْهِمْ رِيحًا صَرْصَرًا فِي يَوْمِ نَحْسٍ مُسْتَمِرٍّ ﴿١٩﴾ تَنْزِعُ النَّاسَ كَأَنَّهُمْ أَعْجَازُ نَخْلٍ مُنْقَعِرٍ ﴿٢٠﴾ فَكَيْفَ كَانَ عَذَابِي وَنُذُرِ ﴿٢١﴾ وَلَقَدْ يَسَّرْنَا الْقُرْآنَ لِلذِّكْرِ فَهَلْ مِنْ مُدَّكِرٍ ﴿٢٢﴾

TRANSLITERATION

18. Kaththabat 'Aadun fakayfa kana 'athabee wanuthur
19. Inna arsalna 'alayhim reehan sarsaran fee yawmi nah-sim-mustamirr
20. Tanzi'u-nnasa ka'annahum a'jazu nakhlim-munqa'ir
21. Fakayfa kana 'athabee wanuthur
22. Walaqad yassarnal-qur'ana liththikri fahal mim-mud-dakir

UNDERSTOOD MEANING

[54:18] 'Aad disbelieved, so how (great) was My punishment and My warning!

[54:19] Surely We sent on them a tornado in a day of continuous curse

[54:20] Tearing men away as if they were the trunks of hollow and torn up palm-trees.

[54:21] How (great) then was My punishment and My warning!

[54:22] And certainly We have made the Qur'an easy for remembrance, but is there anyone who will reflect?

▲ *People in Oman say this is the Tomb of Prophet Hud. It is located near the city of Salalah.*

▲ *A Masjid in Oman*

▲ *Musqat, the capital of Oman*

The Country of Oman

Oman is a Muslim and Arab country in Asia. It is located in the southeastern corner of the Arabian Peninsula. Oman has a long Islamic history. During the eighth year after Hijrah, around 630 AD, Prophet Muhammad sent one of his Sahabah, Amr idn-ul-As, to invite Omanis to Islam. Omanis responded quickly and embraced the new faith. Some historians believe that the 'Aad, the people of Prophet Hud, used to live in Ubar in present Oman. Historians believe that Ubar is the same city of Iram which is mentioned in the Qur'an.

Country Facts

Capital: Muscat

Main Cities: Salalah, Nazwa, Suhar, Soor
Area: 212,500 sq km
Population: 3 million
People: Arab, Asian, African, Baluchi
Language: Arabic, English, Persian
Religion: Muslim
Currency: Omani Riyal

UNIT B   CHAPTER 1

My Beautiful Muslim World

▲ *A beautiful village in Oman*

▲ *An oasis in Oman*

▲ *Inside a palace in Oman*

▲ *An area near Iram (or Ubar)*

Chapter Review

Activity Time

Do some online research about the city of Ubar. Write a journal entry on what you learned about the city of Ubar, and make a collage of pictures on it.

Think Critically

The people of 'Aad were big and tall. They were very strong. Why do you think Allah punished them by sending tornados to blow them around like hollow tree trunks?

Lesson Review

1. What were the people of 'Aad famous for?

   They were famous for houses and

2. The people of 'Aad lived in what present country?

3. Why was Prophet Hud generally respected among his people?

4. What were the first few sentences Prophet Hud said to his people after he was chosen by Allah ﷻ as his prophet?

5. According to the Holy Qur'an, what did Prophet Hud's people say when they heard his message? Why you think they said that?

6. What was the punishment on the people of 'Aad?

7. Who was saved from the punishment?

B11

UNIT B

Prophet Salih
عليه السلام

CHAPTER TWO

Pre-reading Questions

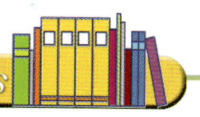

1. Who were the people of Thamood?
2. Who was Prophet Salih?
3. How did Thamood disobey Allah?
4. What was the miracle sent to Thamood?
5. What happened to the disbelievers?

Word Watch

Salih	صالح
Thamood	ثمود
Madain Salih	مَدائِن صالح
Naqah	ناقة

The People of Thamood

Many years passed since the punishment that befell the people of 'Aad. New generations came to succeed them. Among these were the people of Thamood. The people of Thamood ثمود were Arab tribes. They lived in a place now called مدائن صالح Mada'in Salih in the northwestern part of present day

▲ *An ancient house in Mada'in Salih*

▲ *Satellite picture of Arabia, Mada'in Salih is in the far Northwest of Saudi Arabia*

▲ *Ancient houses in Mada'in Salih*

Saudi Arabia. Mada'in Salih is an Arabic name that means "Towns of Salih."

Prophet Salih

The people of Thamood had beautiful gardens. They were blessed with beautiful springs, date palms and trees which had plenty of fruit. They lived in huge houses that they carved out of massive red rocks in the mountains. Allah made them very skillful at carving. The people of Thamood were arrogant, and they oppressed the poor who lived among them.

The people of Thamood moved away from tawheed and started to worship idols. Therefore, Allah ﷻ decided to send them a prophet from amongst themselves to guide them back to the right path. This prophet was صالح عليه السلام Salih. He was a well respected citizen of the people of Thamood. He came from a good family, and was well known for his good character.

Thamood Rejects Allah's Message

"Worship only Allah," Prophet Salih عليه السلام told his people. "You have no other god but Allah, so you should do good. I am giving you good advice: You should believe what I say, for Allah has made me His Prophet." Allah ﷻ reccounts in the Qur'an,

Prophet Salih told his people, "Oh my people! Worship Allah, you have no other god but Him." [Surat-ul-A'raf 7:73]

UNIT B CHAPTER 2

▲ *Ancient houses in Mada'in Salih*

The people of Thamood did not listen to him. They said:

"O Salih! We wished you to be our chief, until you told us to leave our gods and worship your God Alone! We really doubt what you invite us to."

The rich and powerful of the tribe did not listen to Prophet Salih's message. However, many of the wise, poor and humble people followed him. The rich and powerful accused Prophet Salih of being a liar. They said:

"You are nothing but a man, just like any of us. If you are speaking the truth, then show us a proof that you are a prophet." [Surat-ush-Shu'araa' 26:154]

Healthy Habit

Always take the orders of Allah seriously whenever you learn about them; do whatever Allah orders you to do promptly.

The Miracle of the Camel

Prophet Salih prayed to Allah ﷻ to answer their request. Soon afterwards, a mountain moved and split. From it came a giant ناقة naqah, or she-camel, which was pregnant. This camel soon gave birth. Allah ﷻ provided the Thamood people this miracle to prove that Salih was a Prophet. This was also a test from Allah for them, to see if they would obey His orders. Now they didn't have any excuses for not believing in Prophet Salih. The proof they asked for had been brought to them. Prophet Salih عليه السلام told them:

"O my people! This she-camel of Allah is a sign to you. Leave her to feed on Allah's Earth, and do not harm her, or a swift punishment will f"all on you! [11:64]

The she-camel and her young lived among Thamood. Allah ordered Prophet Salih to tell his people of the camel's rights. She would drink from the water of the well for one day, and leave it to them the second day:

"She has a right to drink (water), and you have a right to drink water, each on a day appointed." [Surat-ush-Shu'araa' 26:155]

"And tell them that the water is to be shared between her and them. Each one has the right to drink by turns." [54:28]

On the day the she-camel was to drink from the well, she would have enough milk for all the people of Thamood. They would milk her and fill all their containers. She was so big that when she would graze in the valley the sheep would flee and leave the way for her. The cattle would not come near the well on the day she would drink from it.

The people of Thamood were very amazed by this camel. Therefore, some of them believed in and followed Prophet Salih عليه السلام. It was clear that she was not a normal camel. She was a miracle from Allah and a blessed animal.

The disbelievers, however, were bothered by her a lot because this miracle proved that they were wrong and Salih was a true prophet. They began to accuse the camel of being a danger to their cattle and sheep. These unbelievers began to feel angry and started to feel hatred towards the she-camel and her young one. They could not bear to see them anymore.

Healthy Habit

Always listen to elders and teachers who teach you good things and give you wise advice.

Thamood Kill the Camel and Allah Punishes the Disbelievers

One day, the people of Thamood plotted to kill the camel. That way they could use the well every day. Nine men were appointed to kill the she-camel and her infant. While everyone was asleep, these men went out secretly to do the evil job.

The camel stood up as soon as she saw them, but they hit her on the neck, and she fell to the ground. First they slaughtered her. Then they slaughtered her young. The next day, nobody saw the she-camel or her young. The people searched and found them both dead. When Prophet Salih heard this, he become very angry. Prophet Salih warned them saying:

"Enjoy yourselves in your homes [no more than] three days. This is a promise that will not be belied!" [11:65]

This was a warning for them to repent to Allah ﷻ. Instead, the same nine men decided to kill Prophet Salih as well. They said, "Swear to one another that we shall make a secret night attack on him and his family. Afterwards, we will surely say to his near relatives that we do not know who attacked Salih." Allah ﷻ recounts in the Qur'an:

They said:

"We did not witness the destruction of his family, and we are telling the truth!" [27:48-49]

But Allah ﷻ did not allow them to carry out their plot. As they were going to kill Prophet Salih, Allah showered rocks on them. The nine men were the first to die.

A second day passed after Prophet Salih's warning. Prophet Salih again warned the rest of his people of Allah's punishment that would befall them. The people of Thamood ignored him, and continued to worship their idols. Allah ﷻ instructed Prophet Salih to leave the area with his family and followers.

On the third day, as the sun rose, a terrible Earthquake shook the land. The Earthquake destroyed everything. All the people were destroyed. The area was left barren as if nobody had lived there before! Prophet Salih عليه السلام and his followers were saved from this punishment. He turned away from the dead disbelievers saying:

"O my people! I have indeed delivered to you the message of my Lord, and have given you good advice but you do not like good advisers!" [7:79]

WORDS OF WISDOM
Holy Qur'an

سورة الشمس

Surat-u-Shams

بِسْمِ اللَّهِ الرَّحْمَٰنِ الرَّحِيمِ

وَالشَّمْسِ وَضُحَاهَا ﴿١﴾ وَالْقَمَرِ إِذَا تَلَاهَا ﴿٢﴾ وَالنَّهَارِ إِذَا جَلَّاهَا ﴿٣﴾ وَاللَّيْلِ إِذَا يَغْشَاهَا ﴿٤﴾ وَالسَّمَاءِ وَمَا بَنَاهَا ﴿٥﴾ وَالْأَرْضِ وَمَا طَحَاهَا ﴿٦﴾ وَنَفْسٍ وَمَا سَوَّاهَا ﴿٧﴾ فَأَلْهَمَهَا فُجُورَهَا وَتَقْوَاهَا ﴿٨﴾ قَدْ أَفْلَحَ مَن زَكَّاهَا ﴿٩﴾ وَقَدْ خَابَ مَن دَسَّاهَا ﴿١٠﴾ كَذَّبَتْ ثَمُودُ بِطَغْوَاهَا ﴿١١﴾ إِذِ انبَعَثَ أَشْقَاهَا ﴿١٢﴾ فَقَالَ لَهُمْ رَسُولُ اللَّهِ نَاقَةَ اللَّهِ وَسُقْيَاهَا ﴿١٣﴾ فَكَذَّبُوهُ فَعَقَرُوهَا فَدَمْدَمَ عَلَيْهِمْ رَبُّهُم بِذَنبِهِمْ فَسَوَّاهَا ﴿١٤﴾ وَلَا يَخَافُ عُقْبَاهَا ﴿١٥﴾

TRANSLITERATION

1. Washshamsi waduhaha
2. Waalqamari itha talaha
3. Wannahari itha jallaha
4. Wallayli itha yaghshaha
5. Wassamai wama banaha
6. Wal-Ardi wama tahaha
7. Wanafsin wama sawwaha
8. Fa-alhamaha fujooraha wataqwaha
9. Qad aflaha man zakkaha
10. Waqad khaba man dassaha
11. Kaththabat thamoodu bitaghwaha
12. Ith-inba'atha ashqaha
13. Faqala lahum rasoolullahi naqat-Allahi wasuqyaha
14. Fakaththaboohu faAAaqarooha fadamdama AAalayhim rabbuhum bithanbihim fasawwaha
15. Wala yakhafu 'uqbaha

UNIT B CHAPTER 2

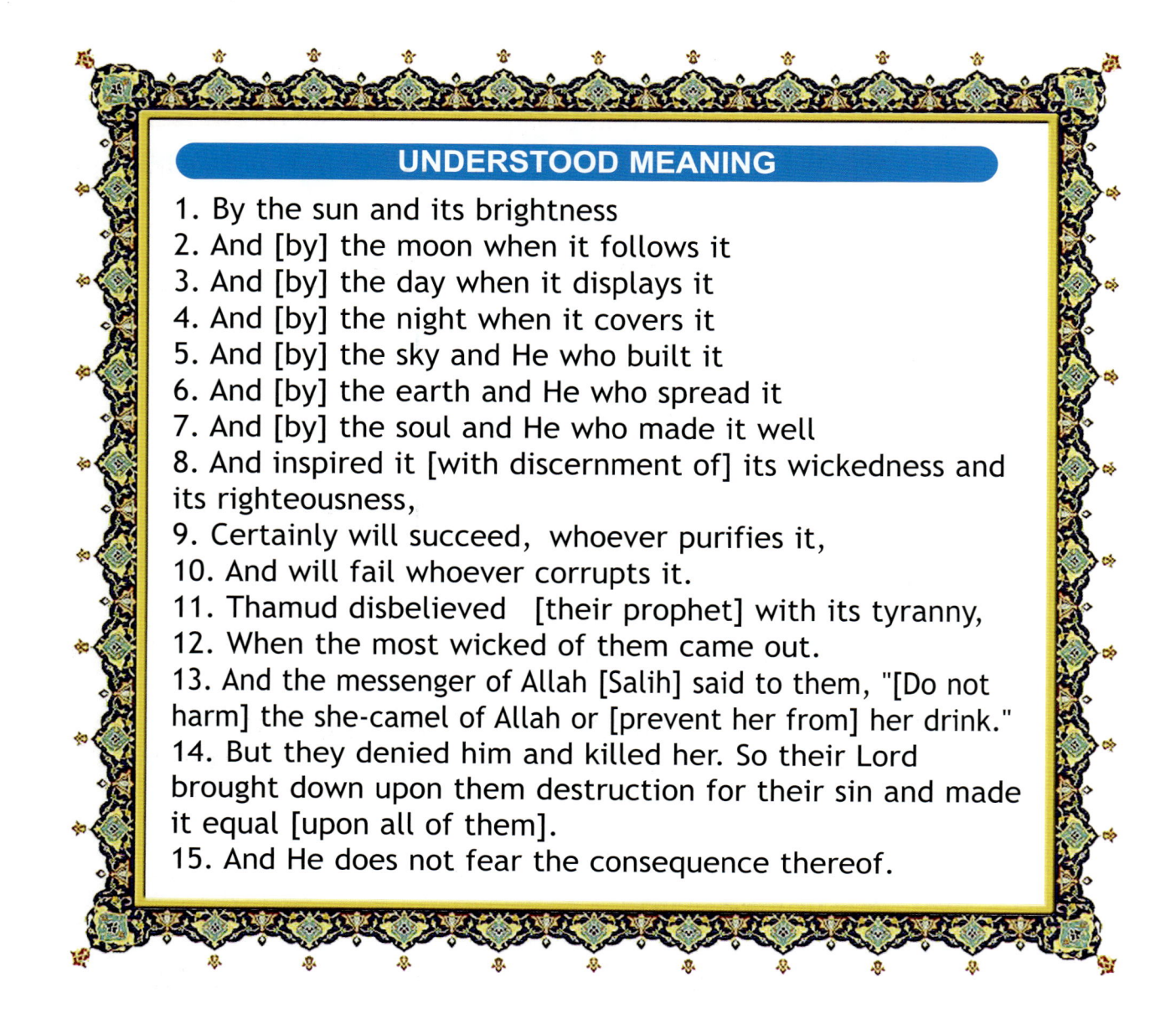

UNDERSTOOD MEANING

1. By the sun and its brightness
2. And [by] the moon when it follows it
3. And [by] the day when it displays it
4. And [by] the night when it covers it
5. And [by] the sky and He who built it
6. And [by] the earth and He who spread it
7. And [by] the soul and He who made it well
8. And inspired it [with discernment of] its wickedness and its righteousness,
9. Certainly will succeed, whoever purifies it,
10. And will fail whoever corrupts it.
11. Thamud disbelieved [their prophet] with its tyranny,
12. When the most wicked of them came out.
13. And the messenger of Allah [Salih] said to them, "[Do not harm] the she-camel of Allah or [prevent her from] her drink."
14. But they denied him and killed her. So their Lord brought down upon them destruction for their sin and made it equal [upon all of them].
15. And He does not fear the consequence thereof.

Activity Time

Write a journal entry on a make believe trip to Mada'in Salih in Saudi Arabia. Describe the place and your feelings about what the people of Thamood did to Prophet Salih and to themselves. You may browse the internet for many pictures, movies and information about Mada'in Salih.

Chapter Review

Think Critically

1. Why do you think the people of Prophet Salih were so rude and arrogant with him?

2. Did the miracle of the camel help Prophet Salih? Explain why?

Lesson Review

1. The people of Thamood came after which people?

2. What were the people of Thamood famous for?

3. What did the people of Thamood worship?

4. Allah ﷻ chose Salih as the prophet for the people of Thamood. According to the Qur'an, what was the first sentence Prophet Salih said to his people?

5. What did the people of Thamood request of Prophet Salih as proof of his prophecy?

6. What was the agreement, according to the Qur'an, regarding the female camel and her infant?

7. What did some of the unbelievers accuse the she-camel and her infant of? What did they do about it?

8. How many days did Prophet Salih give his people to repent to Allah ﷻ?

9. How did Allah protect Prophet Salih from the unbelievers?

10. What was the punishment for the disbelievers among the people of Thamood?

UNIT B

CHAPTER THREE

Prophet Lut and the People of Sodom

Pre-reading Questions

1. Who was Prophet Lut?
2. What were Lut's people like?
3. What happens to people who ignore the truth?

Word Watch

Lut	لوط
Sodom	سَدوم
Dead Sea	البحر الميت

Miss Hibah called on Amir to read the introduction from his book during Islamic Studies class. Amir began reading and the class listened with full attention.

We Love Our Messengers

"Allah's words bring us His Light, Guidance, and Mercy. We should thank Allah for His revelation. We should also appreciate all the efforts of Allah's messengers. They went through many hardships and made many sacrifices so that we could learn the truth. This is why we say '*Sallallahu Alayhi wa Sallam*' or '*alayh-is- salam*' after we say a messenger's name. This means, '*Peace be upon him.*' We Muslims have always wished peace on our prophets and messengers.

"The misguided people, on the other hand, have always tried to hurt or kill the prophets, or to stop the spread of Allah's word. The story of Prophet Lut is one example."

Amir finished reading the section. Miss Hibah divided the class into groups. She told them to read the story in the book individually. She then gave each group a different part of the story to write about. She also said that the groups could draw pictures to go with their part of the story. She would give each group a different part of the story to write about.

The class went to work. For about twenty minutes, the class read the story silently. Then they got into their groups and worked on writing their parts. At the end of the class, each group presented its work.

UNIT B CHAPTER 3

These are the presentations, in order:

Group 1: Bilal as the presenter.

Bilal read, "Lut Ibn Haran عليه السلام was the nephew of Ibraheem. He was one of the messengers sent by Allah. He was sent as a warner to the People of Sadoom, or Sodom, south of the Dead Sea."

Bilal showed the class a map of the Dead Sea from the textbook. This is how it looked:

Bilal continued reading, "The people of Sodom were the worst kind of people in the world. They did all kinds of bad deeds. They used to lie, cheat, steal, drink and

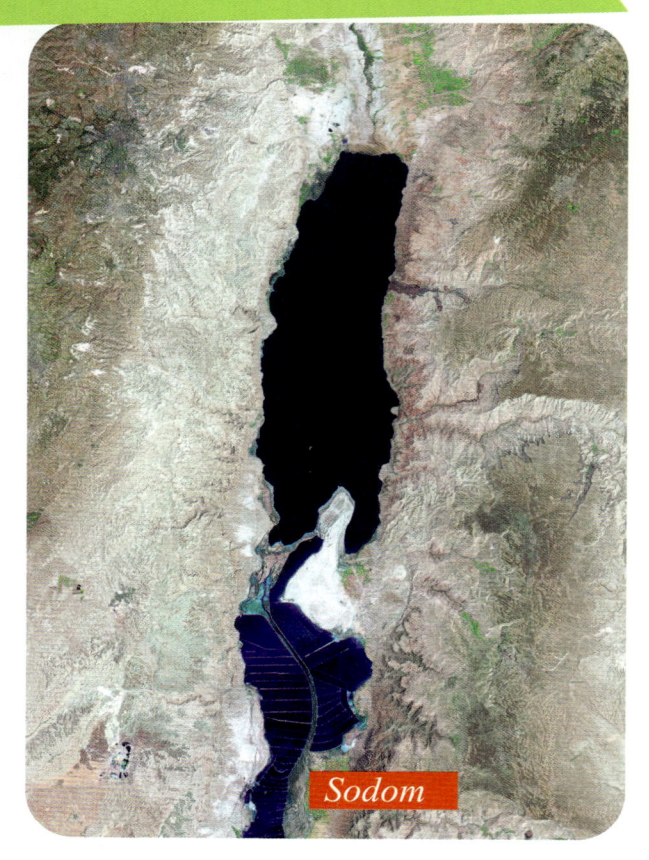

▲ *The City of Sodom, south of the Dead Sea*

do many other shameful acts.

Bilal showed the class some of the pictures that his group drew.

Bilal read more:" Prophet Lut عليه السلام was sent to these people on a mission. He wanted to guide them to the straight path and help them quit their evil actions.

Even though the people of Sodom are called Lut's people, he was not related to them. But he

▲ *Map of Palestine*

looked upon them as his brothers and sisters because he cared about them. He wanted them to go to Jannah.

Bilal finished reading, and Teacher Hibah praised the group. "Very well done, Group 1! Next group!"

Group 2: Mona as the presenter

Mona read, "Prophet Lut عليه السلام was unhappy with the people of Sodom, so he asked them to fear God. He told them that God was the only Lord of the World and they must worship and obey Him alone. Prophet Lut also told them that he was Allah's messenger and they should respect and obey him.

He also asked them to listen, as he gave them good and true advice.

Prophet Lut advised his people to stop committing their terrible sins. He said they must live within Allah's rules. The people disobeyed him and even forbade him to speak. They insisted on being bad. Very few people believed Prophet Lut!

"He warned them that Allah's punishment and anger would be terrible if they did not listen. They challenged Lut." Mona held up a picture that a group member drew.

Mona read on, "Even though the people knew that what they were doing was wrong, they did not stop. Lut spent a long time preaching to them but it made no difference. His people did not believe him and did not listen to his advice. They ignored his warnings and threatened that if he did not stop what he was preaching, they would throw him out of the city.

"Instead of being ashamed of their own deeds, they attacked the good people. They made fun of them for being pure and honest. They acted as if they were good and that the righteous ones were bad." Mona looked up as she finished. Miss Hibah smiled.

B25

"Good job, Group 2. You described how bad the people of Sodom were, and how difficult it was for Prophet Lut to preach to them. Next group!"

Group 3: Zaid as the presenter

Next, Zaid walked up to the front of the classroom. He read, "Lut's people were very difficult to deal with. Not only did they threaten to kick him out of the city, but they challenged him. They did not believe in God or His punishment. They challenged Lut to bring God's punishment to them.

"They said, 'Bring us the wrath of God if you tell the truth.'

They were foolish and ignorant to ask for their own destruction. Prophet Lut was very sad that the people were so blind to the truth. He made dua'a asking God to give him victory over the evil people.

Lut was hurt because his efforts were not working.

"God was displeased by Sodom's insult towards His messenger. He would support His Prophet. God is fair. He sent the people warnings before He punished them. He sent His angels, Jibreel, Israfeel, and Mikaeel on a mission. First, they would visit Prophet Ibraheem and Sarah. Then they would come to Lut."

"After Jibreel, Israfeel, and Mika'eel told Ibraheem and Sarah that they would have another son, Is'haq, they continued their journey. The second part of their mission was to punish the bad people of Sodom. They would also save Prophet Lut and the believers. The angels were disguised as young men as they approached the villages of Sodom. Lut was working in his field. When Lut saw them he knew they were special. They were very handsome. The angels invited themselves in. Lut did not think it was safe for the young men to stay with the people of Sodom because they were evil." This was the end of Zaid's presentation.

Miss Hibah said, "Thank you Group 3. That was a great presentation. Let's see what happened next. Group 4!"

UNIT B CHAPTER 3

Group 4: Khalid as the presenter

Khalid stood in front of the class and began to read. "Prophet Lut felt helpless in front of the angels. He tried to send them away. He warned them that the people of Sodom were probably the worst people on Earth. He repeated himself again and again but the angels were on a mission. They had to follow God's orders, So they stayed with Prophet Lut.

The bad people heard news of the arrival of the handsome young men. They wanted the men to join them in committing their evil sins. They almost went crazy as they attacked Lut's house, trying to snatch away the angels." Khalid showed the class a drawing.

"Lut tried to reason with his people again. The more he advised them, the harder they tried to get to the young men. Lut said, 'Oh Lord! Help me against the people who do mischief. Oh Lord! Protect me and my family from the evil things they do! Oh my people! I wish that I had power to stop you, or that I could have some strong support against you.'"

"Lut felt alone, surrounded by evil men. But he was not alone. Lut had the support of God. His guests were not ordinary men. They were powerful angels. They came to test the people before bringing the punishment to them. The angels now showed Lut who they really were. They told him to leave the city before the morning. In the morning, a horrible punishment would meet the people of Sodom." Khalid was done reading.

Teacher Hibah said, "Jazakum Allahu Khairan, you did a great job Group 4. I will now finish the story for the class. Everyone did an excellent job."

Miss Hibah spoke to the class. "Lut had left Sodom with his family and a few   followers. It is said that Jibreel rooted up the

▲ *Ancient ruins on the shore of the Dead Sea..*

whole village with the tip of his wing, with everything in it, including people, houses, trees, and animals. He lifted it until it reached the sky. The angels could even hear the roosters crow and the dogs bark. Then he flipped it upside down. God's punishment had finally come. He rained down brimstone as hard as baked clay, spreading layer on layer. The showers of brimstone showed that these people were truly wicked, and that they deserved such a punishment."

"Allah replaced the village with a useless lake that had a very foul smell. The people of Sodom became a lesson for the people who wanted to listen. It was a sign of God's inevitable punishment and justice to the evildoers. Allah had destroyed the wicked people and protected His messenger, his family and the few believers who stayed with him."

The class was silent as Miss Hibah finished the story. Miss Hibah let them think quietly for a while. They were thinking about what happens to those who defy Allah and His messengers. They were also thinking how good it was to trust Allah and believe in Him.

B29

WORDS OF WISDOM
Holy Qur'an

سورة القمر

Surat-ul-Qamar 33-40

بِسْمِ اللَّهِ الرَّحْمَٰنِ الرَّحِيمِ

كَذَّبَتْ قَوْمُ لُوطٍ بِالنُّذُرِ ﴿٣٣﴾ إِنَّا أَرْسَلْنَا عَلَيْهِمْ حَاصِبًا إِلَّا ءَالَ لُوطٍ نَّجَّيْنَاهُم بِسَحَرٍ ﴿٣٤﴾ نِّعْمَةً مِّنْ عِندِنَا كَذَٰلِكَ نَجْزِى مَن شَكَرَ ﴿٣٥﴾ وَلَقَدْ أَنذَرَهُم بَطْشَتَنَا فَتَمَارَوْا بِالنُّذُرِ ﴿٣٦﴾ وَلَقَدْ رَاوَدُوهُ عَن ضَيْفِهِ فَطَمَسْنَا أَعْيُنَهُمْ فَذُوقُوا عَذَابِى وَنُذُرِ ﴿٣٧﴾ وَلَقَدْ صَبَّحَهُم بُكْرَةً عَذَابٌ مُّسْتَقِرٌّ ﴿٣٨﴾ فَذُوقُوا عَذَابِى وَنُذُرِ ﴿٣٩﴾ وَلَقَدْ يَسَّرْنَا الْقُرْءَانَ لِلذِّكْرِ فَهَلْ مِن مُّدَّكِرٍ ﴿٤٠﴾

TRANSLITERATION

33. Kaththabat qawmu lootim-binnuthur
34. Inna arsalna 'alayhim hasiban illa aala lootin-najjay-nahum-bisahar
35. Ni'matan min indina kathalika najzee man shakar
36. Walaqad antharahum batshatana fatamaraw binnuthur
37. Walaqad rawadoohu 'an dayfihi fatamasna a'yunahum fathooqoo 'athabee wanuthur
38. Walaqad sabbahahum-bukratan 'athabum-mustaqirr
39. Fathooqoo 'athabee wanuthur
40. Walaqad yassarnal-qur'ana liththikri fahal min-mud-dakir

UNDERSTOOD MEANING

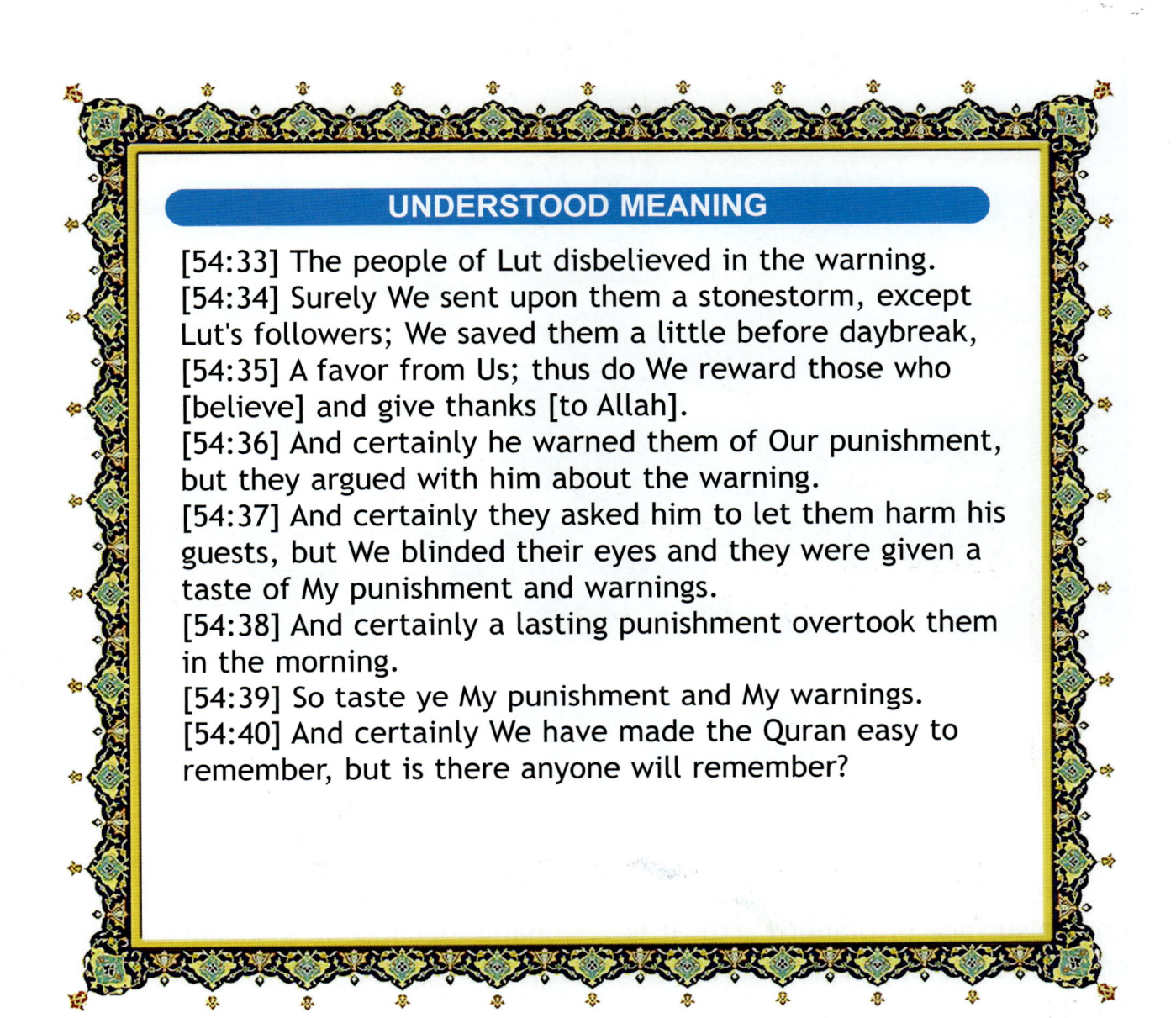

[54:33] The people of Lut disbelieved in the warning.
[54:34] Surely We sent upon them a stonestorm, except Lut's followers; We saved them a little before daybreak,
[54:35] A favor from Us; thus do We reward those who [believe] and give thanks [to Allah].
[54:36] And certainly he warned them of Our punishment, but they argued with him about the warning.
[54:37] And certainly they asked him to let them harm his guests, but We blinded their eyes and they were given a taste of My punishment and warnings.
[54:38] And certainly a lasting punishment overtook them in the morning.
[54:39] So taste ye My punishment and My warnings.
[54:40] And certainly We have made the Quran easy to remember, but is there anyone will remember?

UNIT B CHAPTER 3

▲ The Dead Sea. The lowest and saltiest body of water in the world. Salty rocks can be seen clearly in the picture.

The Dead Sea

The Dead Sea is the lowest point on the surface of planet Earth. It is on the border between the West Bank in Palestine, and Jordan, south of the Jordan River. This body of water is the lowest and the saltiest in the world.

The Dead Sea is about 50 miles long, 11 miles wide and 1200 feet deep at its deepest point.

The Dead Sea has attracted visitors from around the world.

The Dead Sea is called in Arabic البحر الميت Al-Bahr ul-Mayyit, meaning "the Dead Sea." It is given this name because it is so salty, no fish or sea life can live in it. It also used to be called Bahr Lut, meaning "the Sea of Lut" because it is located near Sodom, the area of where the people of Lut used to live.

Chapter Review

Activity Time

1. On the map of Palestine, locate the Dead Sea and the village of Sodom.

Think Critically

1. Why did Allah send the angels to the People of Sodom to give them a punishment, instead of just punishing them right away?

2. How is the story of Lut عليه السلام similar to the story of Prophet Muhammad ﷺ?

Lesson Review

1. Describe the people of Sodom.

2. Where is the village of Sodom located?

3. How did Lut عليه السلام act with his people?

4. How did the wicked people treat Lut?

5. Who visited Prophet Lut in Sodom and what did they tell him?

6. What happened to the people of Sodom?

7. Where is the Dead Sea? How big is it and how deep is it?

B33

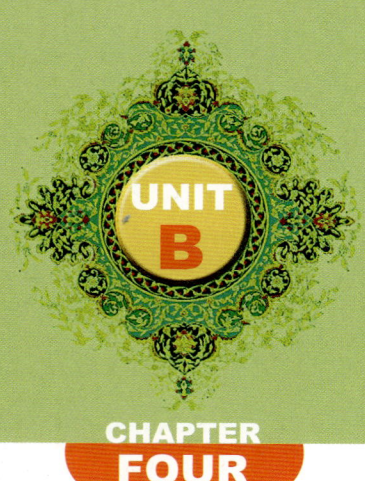

UNIT B
CHAPTER FOUR
Turning to Allah: The Story Of Prophet Younus

Pre-reading Questions

1. What would you do if you were trapped in a small, dark place?
2. Who should you always turn to if you need something?
3. Why did Allah send prophets to His people?

Word Watch

Younus ibn Matta	يونس بن متّى
Naynawa	نينوى
Sabr	صبر
dua'a	دُعاء
Tasbeeh	تسبيح
As-Samee'	السميع

Allah ﷻ loves His servants very much. Allah sent many prophets to show people the right way to Jannah.
One of Allah's prophets was a man called **Younus ibn Matta** عليه السلام.

Allah ﷻ chose **Younus** from among the people to be their prophet. Younus and his people lived in a village called **Naynawa** in Iraq.

Younus عليه السلام started teaching his people Islam. He called on them to worship only one God. They did not want to obey him.

Prophet Younus was afraid for his people because they did not believe in Allah ﷻ. He warned them that if they didn't believe in the One God, they would be punished after three days.

They laughed at Prophet Younus and did not obey him.

Prophet Younus became angry, and he decided to leave the village of Naynawa. He left the village **without getting permission from Allah**. Younus got aboard a ship and sailed away from his people.

While Younus عليه السلام was on the ship,

A STRONG STORM CAME.

The ship was about to sink!!!

People on board started throwing their belongings into the water. They wanted to keep the boat above the water.

The ship was still going to sink.

They thought that the boat would sink because too many people were on it. So they decided to throw at least one person in the water. They made a draw many times, and the name of Younus came up each time! Younus was thrown into the sea.

ALONG CAME A BIG WHALE!

When Prophet Younus was in the water, a big whale came and swallowed him. Allah ordered the whale not to hurt Younus while he was in his stomach.

Now, Prophet Younus was in the stomach of the whale. It was so dark and wet.

Younus was in three types of darkness:

1. He was inside the stomach of the whale

2. He was deep under water.

3. It was night time.
Younus عليه السلام realized that he had left his people without waiting for permission from Allah. He knew he should have been more patient with his people. He started asking Allah for forgiveness and saying that he had been wrong.

It must have been
SO SCARY
for Prophet Younus!

UNIT B CHAPTER 4

The Power of dua'a and Tasbeeh

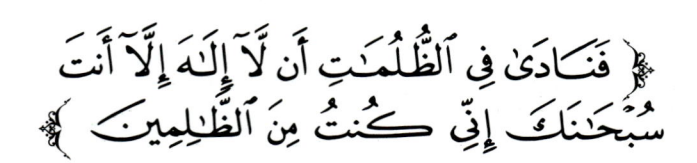

﴿ فَنَادَىٰ فِي ٱلظُّلُمَٰتِ أَن لَّآ إِلَٰهَ إِلَّآ أَنتَ سُبْحَٰنَكَ إِنِّي كُنتُ مِنَ ٱلظَّٰلِمِينَ ﴾

"And he called out within the darknesses, 'There is no God except You; exalted are You. Indeed, I have been of the wrongdoers.'"

Surat-ul-Anbiya'a Ayah 87

I have been wrong.

That was the **dua'a** and **tasbeeh** of Prophet Younus during his days and nights in the whale's stomach. He said it over and over again.

Healthy Habit

When you are upset, sad and need Allah's help, Say:

"لا إله إلا أنت سبحانك إني كنت من الظالمين."

"La ilaha illa anta subhanaka innee kuntu mina-thalimeen."

This means: "There is no God except You; exalted are You. Indeed, I have been of the wrongdoers."

> This time, Prophet Younus learned his lesson and showed **sabr**. This means that he was patient and waited for Allah to do what was best.

Allah heard Prophet Younus's **du'aa'**.

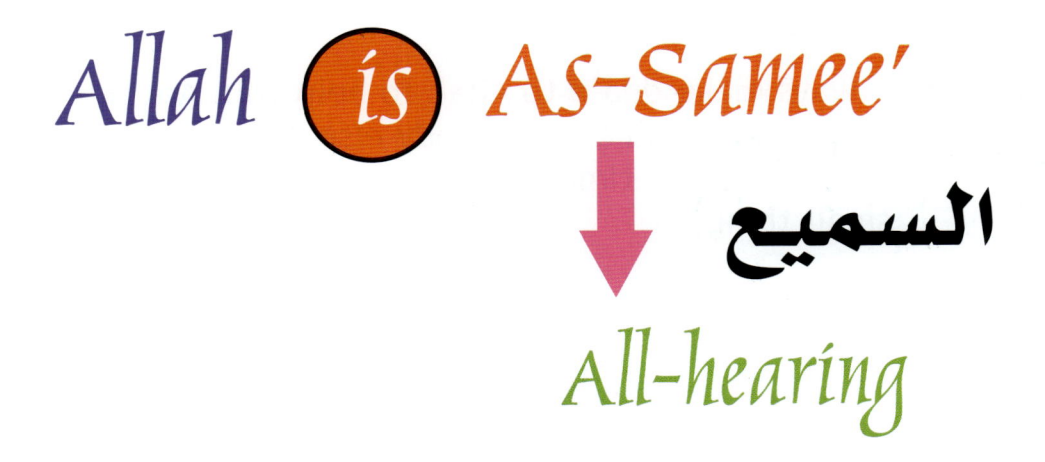

Allah is As-Samee'
السميع
All-hearing

Allah ﷻ made the whale come on shore and spit Younus out of his stomach. Prophet Younus عليه السلام was very sick when he came out.

Allah grew a gourd tree with big leaves over Younus. Now he could eat from its fruit. Younus rested under its big leaves until he became well enough to go back to his people in Naynawa. He began his journey home.

Meanwhile, in the village of Naynawa, a strong wind started. The people were scared.

Now, they knew that Younus was a prophet from Allah.

They were sorry that they had not obeyed Younus, and they began to worship only Allah. Now, all of the people of Naynawa became believers.

They started praying and making dua'a to Allah to stop His punishment and to forgive them.

UNIT B CHAPTER 4

Allah ﷻ is so merciful and forgiving, that He answered their du'aa'.

Allah forgave them and stopped the storm.

Healthy Habit

Always make dua'a to Allah to help you. Ask Him for help before you ask any body else. Make dua'a every day, and every time you need help, even if it is for a small thing.

Do you know how many people lived in the town of Naynawa?

More than 100,000 people!!!

That means there were 100,000 more believers!

This means He answers dua'a and prayers.

When Younus felt better, he returned to Naynawa. To his surprise, all of the people welcomed him! He was so happy.

He started teaching them Islam, and this time, they listened to him.

Chapter Review

Activity Time

1. Draw a whale swimming in the sea under a ship.

2. Write a short paragraph about what you would do if you were in the stomach of the whale.

Think Critically

1. You learned about the story of Prophet Nuh in previous years. Compare and contrast the stories of Prophet Nuh and Prophet Younus.

Lesson Review

1. What did Prophet Younus try to teach his people? At first, did they listen?

2. What did Prophet Younus do when his people disobeyed him? Was this the right thing to do?

3. What happened to Younus in the sea?

4. When Younus realized his mistake, what did he do?

5. How did Allah show Younus that He had forgiven him?

6. When you make a mistake, and need help from Allah, what should you do and say?

Madinah, general view.

Time Line

570 CE		595 CE	610 CE	610-622 CE	1 A.H
Prophet's Birth	Prophet's childhood	Marriage to Khadijah	Prophethood	The difficult times in Makkah	Hijrah

UNIT C: MUSLIMS UNDER SIEGE

CHAPTER 1	Disobedience is Harmful: The Battle of Uhud	**C2**
CHAPTER 2	Searching for the Truth: The Journey of Salman Al-Farisi	**C12**
CHAPTER 3	Surat-ut-Takweer	**C20**
LESSON 1	Surat-ut-Takweer 1	**A20**
LESSON 2	Surat-ut-Takweer 2	**A22**

622 CE	2 A.H. 623 CE	3 A.H. 624 CE	5 A.H. 626 CE
Building Al-Masjid An-Nabawi and establishing Brotherhood	The Battle of Badr	The Battle of Uhud	**The Battle of Al-Khandaq**

UNIT C

CHAPTER ONE

Disobedience is Harmful: The Battle of Uhud

Pre-reading Questions

1. What is Uhud?
2. When was the Battle of Uhud?
3. What caused the Battle of Uhud to happen?

Word Watch

Jabal Uhud — جَبَل أُحُدْ

The Quraysh Want to Take Revenge

Hamzah Ibn Abdul Muttalib, the uncle of the Prophet, was concerned about the news he heard from Makkah. Al-Abbas, the other uncle of the Prophet, sent a message from Makkah that the Quraysh were marching a big army toward Madinah. Al-Abbas was not a Muslim at that time, but used to care about the Prophet and the Muslims. The Quraysh wanted to avenge their defeat in Badr and destroy the Muslims once and for all. For that cause, they prepared a big army of 3000 fighters and set out for Madinah.

C2

▲ *Jabal Uhud in Madinah.*

All of the Quraysh's men, women, and their slaves went to war under the leadership of Abu-Sufyan. Their targets were mainly two men—Muhammad and Hamzah. They hired a slave who was skilled in throwing the javelin. His name was "Wahshi," the slave of Jubair Ibn Mut'im, who was killed in Badr. They promised him his freedom. Hind bint Utbah who lost her father and brother in Badr, offered him her jewelry. Hind was also the wife of Abu Sufyan, the leader of Quraysh. To her, Hamzah was the killer of her father.

Planning for the Battle

The Prophet found himself with only 700 Muslims to fight 3,000 of the Quraysh. As in Badr, the enemies were many times more numerous than the Muslims. Rasoolullah asked his companions whether to fight the enemies inside or outside Madinah. In opposition to the Prophet's opinion, most of the sahabah wanted to fight the enemy outside the city walls. Many of them missed Badr and wanted to experience jihad and defend Islam.

Unlike the rest of the Sahabah, the Prophet ﷺ felt it was safer to stay in Madinah. He hoped that no fight would take place. Even if fighting became necessary, it would be harder for the enemy to fight the Muslims in their home town. Muslims, he thought, knew the backstreets and allies better. He thought that Muslims could use the roofs and their little forts to their advantage. The Prophet ﷺ also had a vision the night before the battle. He figured out from the vision that staying in Madinah was safer. However, the Prophet yielded to the opinion of the majority of Muslims.

Getting Ready for the Battle

To meet the threat, the Prophet, with a batch of 700 men, took up position at the foot of Mount Uhud. All sincere Muslims came and joined the Muslim army. Even young boys wanted to join and defend Islam. However, due to their tender age, the Prophet turned down 'Usamah Ibn Zaid, Abdullah Ibn Umar Ibn-ul-Khattab, Zaid Ibn Thabit, Al-Bara' Ibn 'Azib, 'Amr Ibn Hazm and many others.

The Prophet ﷺ chose his position so that mount Uhud was at his back. He positioned his men in battle array and gave the banner to Mus'ab Ibn 'Umair. He also put 50 archers under the leadership of

Abdullah Ibn Jubair and kept them on a hill near Mount Uhud. Rasoolullah told them to repel the horses with their arrows. He gave them a very clear command to stay on the hill until they received another order.

The Quraysh army marched to Madinah during the month of Shawwal, in the 3rd year after Hijrah. The Quraysh's force camped at Mount Uhud, some three miles from Madinah. They arranged their army facing the Muslim troops. Khalid Ibn-ul-Waleed was on the right flank and led their cavalry. Talhah Ibn Abu-Talhah was the standard bearer of the Quraysh's army and Abu-Sufyan was their commander.

The Prophet ﷺ offered his sword to Abu-Dujanah and told him: "Strike the enemy till the sword is bent."

The Battle Heats Up

Hamzah was in the center of the battleground. He was wearing his armor and swooping on the enemy from all directions. All Muslims fought bravely and worked as one team. They were winning the battle in the beginning. When they saw the enemy fleeing, they thought the battle was over. Some archers disobeyed the Prophet ﷺ and left their post to chase the fleeing army. They hoped to collect some spoils. In doing that, they left a gap in the lines of the Muslim army.

All of a sudden, the enemy cavalry, led by Khalid Ibn Al-Walid, surprised them from behind and came through that gap. They went up the hill of archers and killed the archers who still remained at their posts, then attacked the Muslim army from behind. Then confusion threw the Muslims off balance. The fleeing enemy army rebounded, killing a great number of Muslim soldiers.

As a test from God the victory changed into defeat. Khalid Ibn Al-Waleed came from behind, 'Ikrimah came from the other flank and the fleeing Abu-Sufyan from the front. The Muslims were surrounded on all sides.

Chaos prevailed while the Muslims tried to retrieve their swords. They were so confused that they no longer knew their friends from their foes.

▲ The Hill of Archers: This is the hill where the Prophet ordered the archers to take position.

Hamzah Martyred

Hamzah saw what had happened, but did not panic. He stood his ground and doubled his efforts in fighting. Hamzah and Abu-Dujanah bravely fell on the enemy and attacked every fighter who came their way. Hamzah fought and killed the banner carrier of the Quraysh. Abu-Dujanah saw a person who was fiercely shouting amongst the Quraysh. He drew his sword to kill him, but it was a woman, Hind. He did not want to disgrace the sword of the Prophet ﷺ by killing a woman. That is something the Prophet did not approve of.

Watching Hamzah closely was Wahshi, the slave to whom Hind promised his freedom and her jewelry. He was waiting for the right moment. He spotted Hamzah swooping on the people with his mighty sword, nothing stopping him. Wahshi, hiding behind a tree trunk, prepared his javelin. He never missed. And this time he was after the grand prize, his freedom. He saw Hamzah the chasing down a fighter from Quraysh to kill him. Wahshi aimed his javelin with a firm grip, and made sure of his aim. Was sure he would not miss, he threw the javelin and it pierced Hamzah's body. Hamzah advanced a few steps forward, but under the severe blow, his body fell to the ground. Asadu Allah, or the Lion of Allah, as the Prophet called him, was martyred. He had lived a great life and his death was honorable too. The slave snatched his javelin, after making sure that Hamzah was dead, and hurried to Hind to collect his reward.

The Prophet in Danger

After Hamzah was killed, the enemy focused on the Prophet. The disbelievers advanced towards the Prophet. He was pelted with stones that broke his tooth and wounded his face and lip. He bled, and as he was wiping it, he said, "How could people cut open the face of their Prophet, while he invites them to worship their God alone?"

The Prophet ﷺ, with about 12 men, was surrounded by the enemy. Mus'ab Ibn 'Umair took up the banner of Islam and stationed himself near the Prophet. Ibn Qumay'ah Laithi attacked Mus'ab, who was carrying the banner. When Mus'ab was killed, the banner dropped from his hand. 'Ali took over as bearer.

Thinking that he had killed the Prophet ﷺ, Ibn Qumay'ah Laithie climbed up a hill and shouted, "Muhammad has been killed!" The disbelievers were overjoyed and the Muslims were dumbstruck.

But Ka'b Ibn Malik, who was close to the Prophet, shouted: "Oh Muslims! Be happy, for the Prophet of God is alive. Come here."

The Prophet himself shouted at the top of his voice, "Towards me, you servants of God! I am the Messenger of God."

The End of the Battle

In an instant, both friends and foes rushed towards the Prophet. However, the enemy arrived first. They were numerous and the Muslims dispersed. The Prophet ﷺ was wounded and lost a tooth, but God's help was near. The devoted companions rushed to the place, giving and receiving blows. Every one of them had serious wounds. They formed a barricade around the Prophet.

Abu- Dujanah, who fought hard with the Prophet's sword, came up and covered the Prophet's ﷺ holy body with his own. He exposed his broad back to the hail of enemy's arrows. S'ad Ibn Abi-Waqass, Abu-Talha, Zubair and 'Abdur Rahman Ibn 'Auwf shielded the Prophet by making a human wall around him, receiving sword wounds on their arms. Ziyad Ansari and five of his companions gave their lives defending the Prophet ﷺ. Even a woman, Naseebah bint Ka'b, known also as Ummu-Omarah, had her arm hurt by Ibn Qumay'ah while trying to save the Prophet from his attackers.

The fight continued fiercely. Gradually the Muslims, with unmatched courage and under the most difficult of circumstances, repelled the attack of the enemy and forced them back.

The danger was not over yet. Ubbay Ibn Khalaf had vowed to kill the Prophet on a special horse which he had groomed especially for the occasion. He was riding it and advancing to fulfill his vow. The Prophet asked his companions to let him approach. When he was close enough, the Prophet took a spear and aimed it at 'Ubbay's neck. 'Ubay tilted violently on his horse. He turned his back and fled, but that wound proved fatal. That last effort of the Prophet ﷺ renewed the courage of the Muslims and disheartened the disbelievers. The disbelievers became exhausted and gave up the attack. Abu Sufyan felt that the Quraysh had won the battle and wanted to keep it that way. He knew it would be difficult to actually kill the Prophet and destroy the Muslims. When the fight slowed down, the Muslims stood guard around the Prophet at Mount Uhud.

▲ *The graves of Hamzah and other Martyrs near mount Uhud surrrounded by the white walls.*

Abu Sufyan then shouted: "Hubal is high today (Quraysh's main idol)!"

The Prophet ordered Omar to respond, "Allah is higher and has all the glory."

Abu Sufyan shouted again: "Oh Muhammad, this day is for the day of Badr."

The Prophet ordered Omar to respond and say: "It is not the same; our martyrs are in Jannah, whereas your dead are in hell fire."
Then Abu Sufyan and his army left to Makkah.

Lessons Learned

The archers left a gap in their flank which allowed the disbelievers to approach the battlefield from behind and surprise the Muslims. Victory was turned into defeat. This is exactly what disobedience of Allah and His Prophet does to individuals and societies. It was the will of Allah to test the believers in victory and in defeat.

On that day the Muslims learned a bitter lesson very well. The Prophet didn't blame the archers or make things hard on them. Everyone knew what had happened, learned a lesson about obeying authority, and made sure to act more responsibly in the future.

Healthy Habit

Always obey Allah, the Prophet, your parents, your teachers and authority.
Avoid causing your team or family trouble by disobeying their rules and instructions.

Chapter Review

Activity Time

1. Create a collage of pictures of Madinah and Jabal Uhud.
2. Write a short poem about the Battle of Uhud.

Think Critically

1. Suppose you had been with the Prophet when he was trying to decide where to engage the enemy. Which way would you have voted? Why?
2. Suppose you had been one of the archers. Some of them decided to leave their posts while others insisted on staying as the Prophet had instructed. What would you have done and why?
3. Why do you think the enemy tried its best to kill the Prophet?

Lesson Review

1. What is Uhud and where is it?
2. What was the main cause of the Battle of Uhud?
3. Briefly answer the following questions:
    a. When did the Battle of Uhud take place?
    b. Who was the leader of the Muslim army?
    c. Where did the Battle of Uhud take place?
    d. Who was the leader of Quraysh's army?
    e. Who was the banner bearer of the Muslims?
    f. Who killed Hamzah? Who killed Mus'ab Ibn Omair?
    g. Who did the Prophet kill in the Battle of Uhud?
    h. Who was the leader of the archers?
    i. Who was the woman who defended the Prophet at Uhud?
4. What were the Prophet's instructions to the archers?
5. Describe how the Sahabah defended the Prophet?
6. What did Abu Sufyan say to the Muslims at the end of the battle, and what was the Prophet's response to him?

UNIT C
CHAPTER TWO

Searching for the Truth: The Journey of Salman Al-Farisi

Pre-reading Questions

1. Who was Salman Al-Farisi?
2. Do you know any stories about him?
3. Can you quote a hadeeth about this great man?

Word Watch

Salman the Persian	سلمان الفارسي
Esfahan	أصفهان

Salman Al-Farisi

Salman Al-Farisi was a great young man from Persia during the time of Prophet Muhammad. Persia was the old name for Iran. He was born in the city of Esfahan. Salman was not happy with what his people used to do because they were fire worshippers. Many of the Persian people were Magian, or Majoos, and thought the fire was God. Let us listen to the story of Salman Al-Farisi, or Salman the Persian, as he tells it.

I was a Persian boy from a tribe called "Jian." My father was a leader of the village and one of the richest people

A Mosque in Esfahan, Iran

there. He loved me so much and always took care of me. My family used to worship fire. They raised me to serve the temple in the village and I became the guardian of the fire that we worshipped. I was in charge of kindling it, so that it would not die out.

The Curious Young Man

One day I saw a church and heard Christians praying there. This caught my curiosity. I knew nothing about Christianity. So I entered the church to see what they did. Their prayer attracted me and I thought about following their religion. I felt it was better than my Magian religion. I stayed there until sunset and I asked the people in the church where their religion came from. They told me that it began in ancient Syria.

When I returned home that night, my father asked me, "Where were you all day?" I told him the whole story. My father became very worried when I told him that Christianity was better than our religion. He locked me up and shackled my legs to stop me from going to the church.

Looking for the True Faith

"I sent a message to some Christians asking them to help me. I managed to get rid of my shackles and escaped to Syria. When I arrived there, I asked about the most knowledgeable man in Christianity. The people there guided me to a monk. I told him that I wanted to become Christian, serve him, and worship with him. He agreed.

Shortly afterwards, I discovered that he was a bad man. He received gold and silver as charity. Instead of giving it to the poor, he kept it for himself in seven sacks. This made me hate him very much. When he died, I told the people about his evil actions and showed them where he kept their gold and silver. They became very angry with him. They crucified his corpse and threw stones at it.

The people selected a new and better monk. I loved him very much and spent a long time with him. He was a true and sincere worshipper of God. When he was about to die, I asked him, whom should I follow after his death. He advised me to go to a man in Mosul in north Iraq. I went to Mosul and stayed with that monk until he died.

Before his death I asked him, whom I should follow after him. He advised me to go to a man in Nasibeen. So I traveled to Nasibeen and stayed with the monk there until he died. On his death bed I asked him about whom I should follow after his death. He advised me to go to a man in `Ammouriyyah, in present day Turkey. I went there and met him. During my stay there I worked and owned a sheep and a number of cows.

The Promised Prophet

"The monk of Ammouriyyah was old and ill. When he was about to die, I asked him whom I should follow after him. He told me that were no longer any followers of true Christianity. He sadly said,
"I don't know of a living person who follows the true religion of Jesus, the son of Mary, peace be upon him. However, to the best of my knowledge, in this era, a Messenger of God will appear in Arabia. He will come to a place of palm trees between two rocky lands. He will teach God's message to all peoples. After I die, stay here at my hut, and look for the traveling caravans from Arabia. Ask Arab merchants whether a prophet has appeared among them lately. If they answer "yes," then this is the one. Jesus, peace be upon

him, said he would come after him.

There are signs that will tell you he is a prophet. Among his signs, you will see the Seal of Prophethood on his back, between his shoulders. He accepts and eats from gifts, and he does not eat from charity."

Salman continued: "After the man died, I stayed in his hut and whenever a caravan passed by, I asked, 'What land do you come from?' Finally, one day, a caravan from Makkah came by, and when they told me that they were from the Hijaz, I asked, 'Has there appeared among you someone who says he is a prophet?'

They replied, 'Yes, indeed!' I asked them to take me with them to the Arab land in return for the sheep and cows I had.

When the caravan reached Makkah, the men betrayed me and sold me to a Jewish man there. The Jew then sold me to his cousin, who took me to his hometown, Yathrib. I saw there the palm trees and remembered the prophecy which the monk of `Ammouriayah told me. Meanwhile, the Prophet ﷺ began his call in Makkah, but I knew nothing about him because I was a slave and very busy doing many things for my master.

Meeting Prophet Muhammad

After the Prophet ﷺ migrated to Medinah, I wanted to see if he was a true prophet. So, I went to him with some dates and offered it to him as sadaqah, or charity. He gave the dates to some of his companions but he did not eat any. I became sure of the first sign of his prophecy. I again brought him some dates and offered them to him as a present. He ate from them and gave same to his companions. I became sure of the second sign of prophecy.

One day I went to the Messenger in Al-Baqee', the grave yard of Madinah. I wanted to see if he had the Seal of Prophethood on his back. After he had buried a dead man, I offered him greetings. I then turned to his back trying to see the Seal of Prophethood. He understood what I wanted and let me see it. When I saw the seal, I started kissing him and crying. The Messenger ﷺ asked me, "What is the matter with you?" I told him the whole story. He was amazed by it and told me to retell it again to his companions.

Becoming a Muslim

Salman continued, "From that day on, I accepted Islam and stayed in Prophet Muhammad's company until the end." rasoolullah helped Salman to regain his freedom and he became one of the great Sahabah.

rasoolullah ﷺ was the kindest of all people in the whole world. He always took care of his companions and the people around him. Once he noticed that Salman felt like a stranger, being a Persian among Arabs in Madinah. So he declared to all people in Madinah:

سَلْمَان مِنْ آلِ البَيْتِ

Salman is part of my family

The Prophet indeed used to love and respect Salman because he was a true believer and great searcher for the truth. It was reported that the Prophet ﷺ one day put his hands on Salman and said, "If faith was high up in the stars, some men like that (pointing to Salman) would have attained it."

C17

Story Time

When Salman Al-Farisi embraced Islam, the Prophet established brotherhood between Salman and Abud-Dardaa', one of the kindest Sahabah. Salman went to stay with Abud-Dardaa' and found Ummud-Dardaa', his wife, dressed in shabby clothes. He asked her why she was dressed so poorly. She said, "Abud-Dardaa' is not interested in this dunya."

Then Abud-Dardaa' came and prepared a meal for Salman, but didn't eat with him. Salman asked Abud-Dardaa' to join him, but Abu Ad-Dardaa' said, "I am fasting." (That was an optional fast). Salman then said, "I am not eating until you eat." So, Abud-Dardaa' ate. When it was midnight, Abud-Dardaa' got up to pray Qiyam-ul-Layl. Salman told him to sleep and Abud-Darda' slept. When it was the last hour of the night, Salman told him to get up then, and both prayed together.

Salman told Abud-Dardaa', "Your Lord has a right on you, your body has a right on you, and your wife and family have rights on you; so you should repect the rights of all those who have a right on you." This means that the Muslim should not neglect the needs of his body and family.

Abud-Dardaa' came to the Prophet and told him the whole story. The Prophet ﷺ said, "Salman has spoken the truth."

This story is reported in Saheeh-ul-Bukhari.

Chapter Review

Activity Time

Draw a map of Iran and point out the cities of Tehran and Esfahan.

Think Critically

1. Islam is against racism. How can you prove that by using the story of Salman Al-Farisi?

2. Do you think Salman would have become a great Muslim if he had not been serious in his search for the truth? Explain your answer.

Lesson Review

1. Where was Salman Al-Farisi from?

2. What was the thing Salman was searching for when he was young?

3. Why do think he was looking for that thing?

4. What religion did Salman follow before Islam?

5. What were the signs of prophethood he learned from the monk of Ammouriyyah?

6. Quote one hadeeth about Salman.

UNIT C CHAPTER 3 LESSON ONE

Surat-ut-Takweer 1

WORDS OF WISDOM
Holy Qur'an

سورة التكوير

Surat-ut-Takweer 1-14

﴿إِذَا ٱلشَّمْسُ كُوِّرَتْ ۝١ وَإِذَا ٱلنُّجُومُ ٱنكَدَرَتْ ۝٢ وَإِذَا ٱلْجِبَالُ سُيِّرَتْ ۝٣ وَإِذَا ٱلْعِشَارُ عُطِّلَتْ ۝٤ وَإِذَا ٱلْوُحُوشُ حُشِرَتْ ۝٥ وَإِذَا ٱلْبِحَارُ سُجِّرَتْ ۝٦ وَإِذَا ٱلنُّفُوسُ زُوِّجَتْ ۝٧ وَإِذَا ٱلْمَوْءُۥدَةُ سُئِلَتْ ۝٨ بِأَيِّ ذَنۢبٍ قُتِلَتْ ۝٩ وَإِذَا ٱلصُّحُفُ نُشِرَتْ ۝١٠ وَإِذَا ٱلسَّمَآءُ كُشِطَتْ ۝١١ وَإِذَا ٱلْجَحِيمُ سُعِّرَتْ ۝١٢ وَإِذَا ٱلْجَنَّةُ أُزْلِفَتْ ۝١٣ عَلِمَتْ نَفْسٌ مَّآ أَحْضَرَتْ ۝١٤﴾

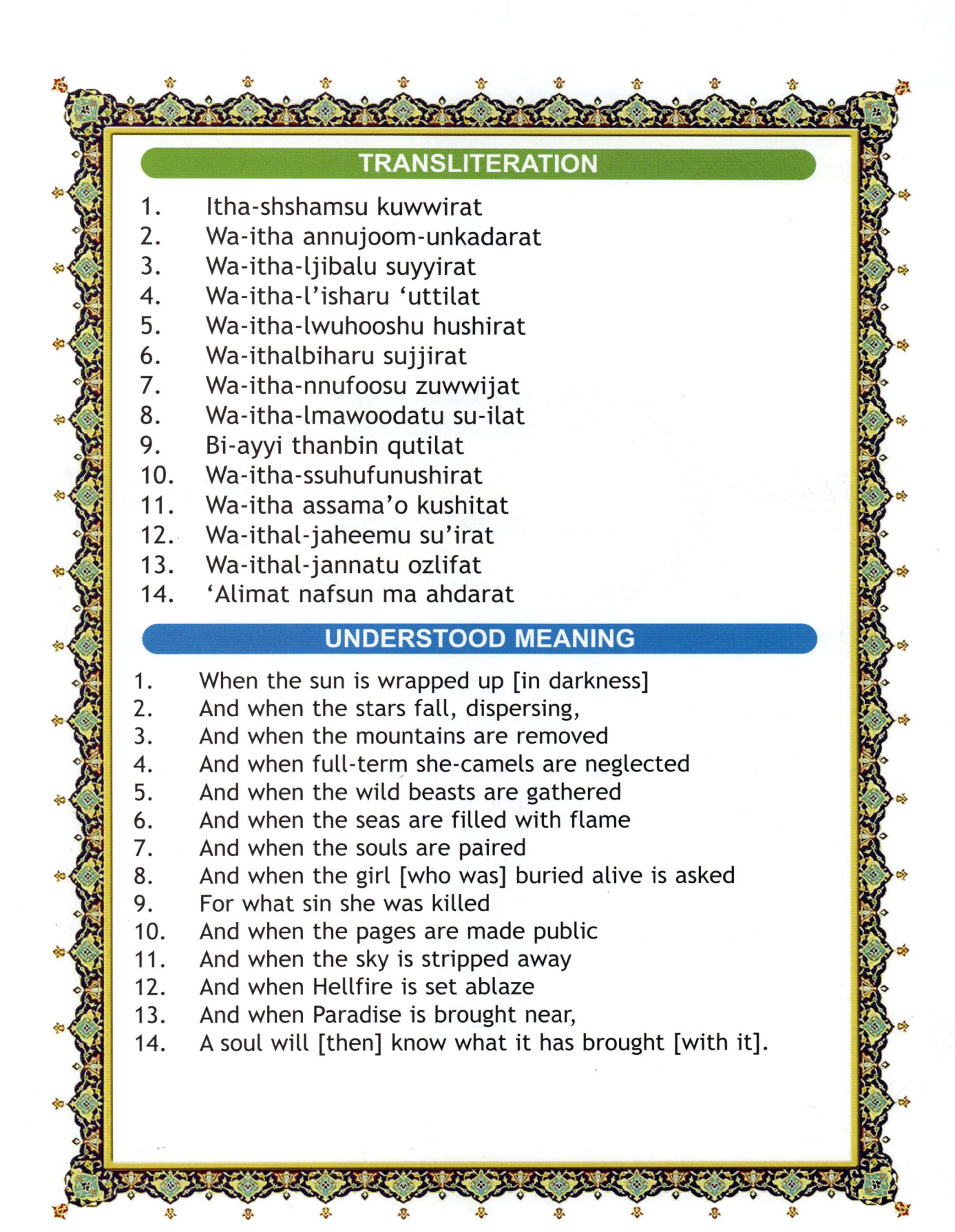

TRANSLITERATION

1. Itha-shshamsu kuwwirat
2. Wa-itha annujoom-unkadarat
3. Wa-itha-ljibalu suyyirat
4. Wa-itha-l'isharu 'uttilat
5. Wa-itha-lwuhooshu hushirat
6. Wa-ithalbiharu sujjirat
7. Wa-itha-nnufoosu zuwwijat
8. Wa-itha-lmawoodatu su-ilat
9. Bi-ayyi thanbin qutilat
10. Wa-itha-ssuhufunushirat
11. Wa-itha assama'o kushitat
12. Wa-ithal-jaheemu su'irat
13. Wa-ithal-jannatu ozlifat
14. 'Alimat nafsun ma ahdarat

UNDERSTOOD MEANING

1. When the sun is wrapped up [in darkness]
2. And when the stars fall, dispersing,
3. And when the mountains are removed
4. And when full-term she-camels are neglected
5. And when the wild beasts are gathered
6. And when the seas are filled with flame
7. And when the souls are paired
8. And when the girl [who was] buried alive is asked
9. For what sin she was killed
10. And when the pages are made public
11. And when the sky is stripped away
12. And when Hellfire is set ablaze
13. And when Paradise is brought near,
14. A soul will [then] know what it has brought [with it].

UNIT C CHAPTER 3 LESSON TWO

Surat-ut-Takweer 2

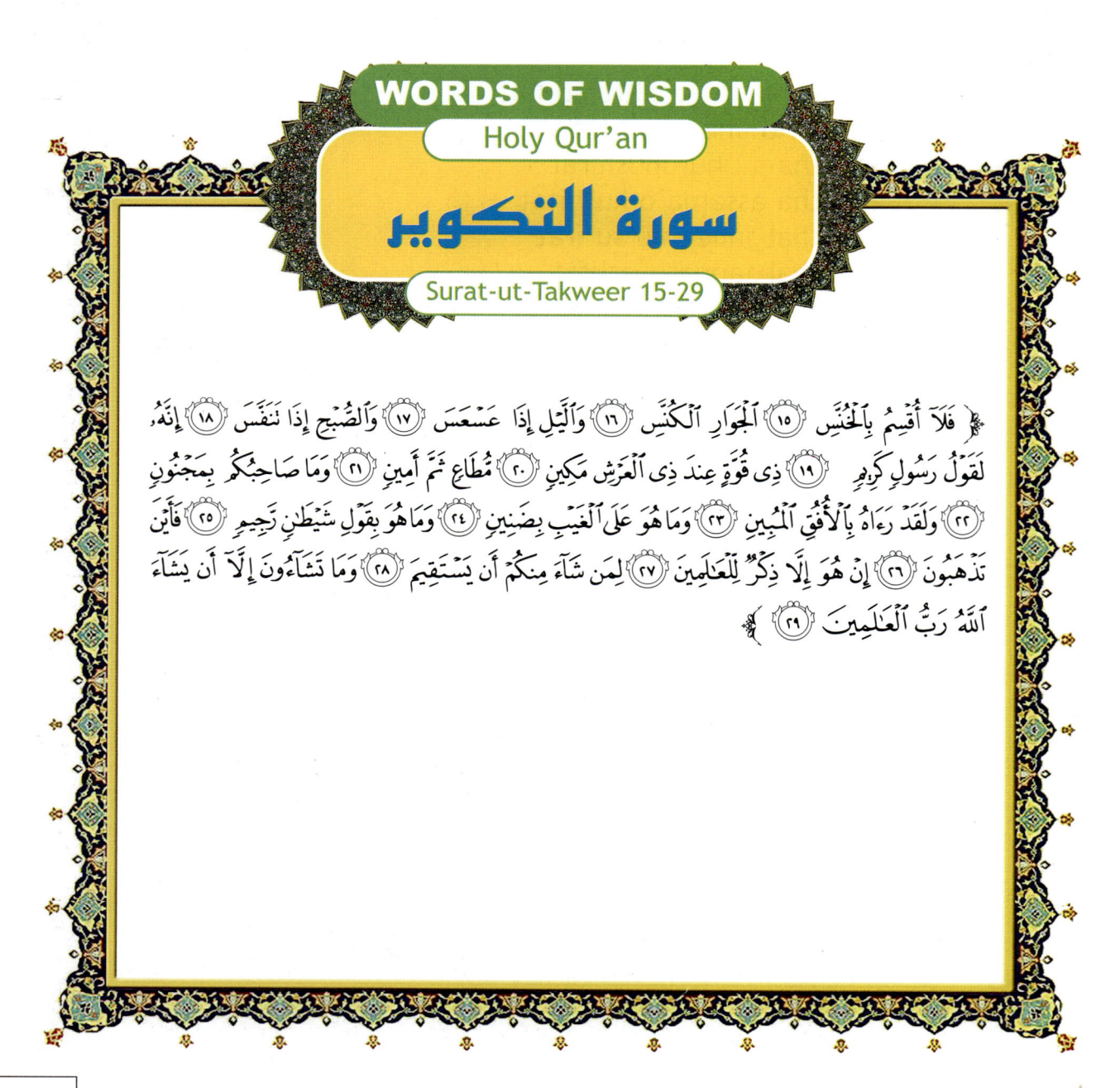

WORDS OF WISDOM
Holy Qur'an

سورة التكوير

Surat-ut-Takweer 15-29

فَلَا أُقْسِمُ بِالْخُنَّسِ ﴿١٥﴾ الْجَوَارِ الْكُنَّسِ ﴿١٦﴾ وَاللَّيْلِ إِذَا عَسْعَسَ ﴿١٧﴾ وَالصُّبْحِ إِذَا تَنَفَّسَ ﴿١٨﴾ إِنَّهُ لَقَوْلُ رَسُولٍ كَرِيمٍ ﴿١٩﴾ ذِي قُوَّةٍ عِندَ ذِي الْعَرْشِ مَكِينٍ ﴿٢٠﴾ مُطَاعٍ ثَمَّ أَمِينٍ ﴿٢١﴾ وَمَا صَاحِبُكُم بِمَجْنُونٍ ﴿٢٢﴾ وَلَقَدْ رَآهُ بِالْأُفُقِ الْمُبِينِ ﴿٢٣﴾ وَمَا هُوَ عَلَى الْغَيْبِ بِضَنِينٍ ﴿٢٤﴾ وَمَا هُوَ بِقَوْلِ شَيْطَانٍ رَجِيمٍ ﴿٢٥﴾ فَأَيْنَ تَذْهَبُونَ ﴿٢٦﴾ إِنْ هُوَ إِلَّا ذِكْرٌ لِّلْعَالَمِينَ ﴿٢٧﴾ لِمَن شَاءَ مِنكُمْ أَن يَسْتَقِيمَ ﴿٢٨﴾ وَمَا تَشَاءُونَ إِلَّا أَن يَشَاءَ اللَّهُ رَبُّ الْعَالَمِينَ ﴿٢٩﴾

TRANSLITERATION

15. Fala oqsimu bilkhunnas
16. Aljawaril-kunnas
17. Wallayli itha 'as'as
18. Wassubhi itha tanaffas
19. Innahu laqawlu rasoolin kareem
20. Thee quwwatin 'inda thil 'arshi makeen
21. Muta'in thamma ameen
22. Wama sahibukum bimajnoon
23. Walaqad raahu bil-ofuq-il-mubeen
24. Wama huwa 'alal-ghaybi bidaneen
25. Wama huwa biqawli shaytanin rajeem
26. Fa ayna tathhaboon
27. In huwa illa thikrun lil-'alameen
28. Liman sha'a minkum an yastaqeem
29. Wama tasha'oona illa an yasha'-Allahu rabbul-'alameen

UNDERSTOOD MEANING

15. So I swear by the retreating stars -
16. Those that run [their courses] and disappear -
17. And by the night as it closes in
18. And by the dawn when it breathes
19. [That] indeed, the Qur'an is a word [conveyed by] a noble messenger
20. [Who is] possessed of power and with the Owner of the Throne, secure [in position],
21. Obeyed there [in the heavens] and trustworthy.
22. And your companion is not [at all] mad.
23. And he has already seen Gabriel in the clear horizon.
24. And Muhammad is not a withholder of [knowledge of] the unseen.
25. And the Qur'an is not the word of a devil, expelled [from the heavens].
26. So where are you going?
27. It is not except a reminder to the worlds
28. For whoever wills among you to take a right course.
29. And you do not will except that Allah wills - Lord of the worlds.

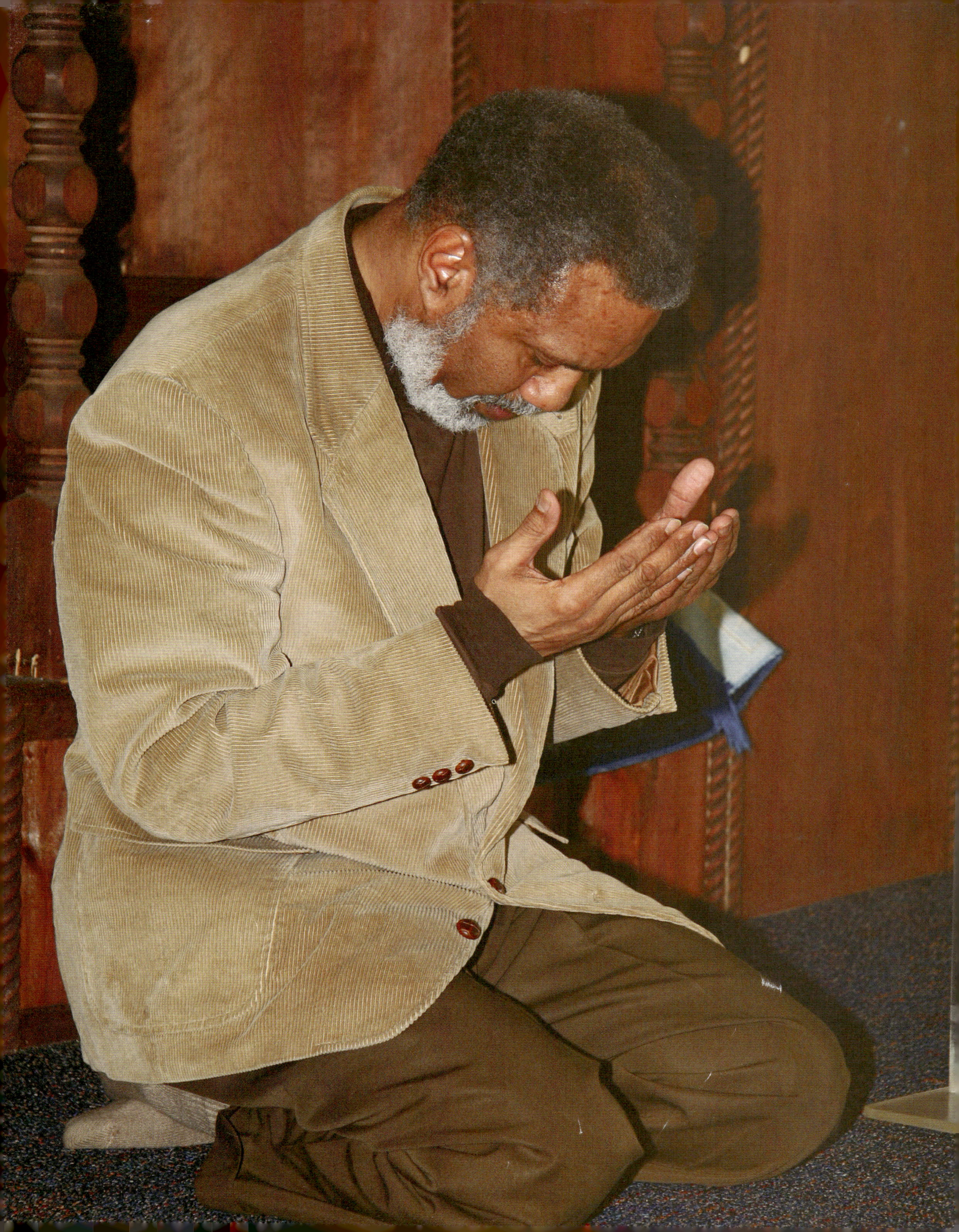

UNIT D: WORSHIP WITH HEART

CHAPTER 1	Al-Khushoo': The Heart of Worship	D2
CHAPTER 2	Salat-ul-Jama'ah: A Prayer Allah loves	D10
CHAPTER 3	How To Pray Salat-ul-Jama'ah	D16
CHAPTER 4	Salat-ul-Jumu'ah: The Friday Prayer	D22
CHAPTER 5	Appreciating Allah's Gifts	D30
CHAPTER 6	Sujood-ush-Shukr	D38
CHAPTER 7	Zakah: The Third Pillar of Islam	D46

UNIT D

Al Khushoo' the Heart of Worship

CHAPTER ONE

Pre-reading Questions

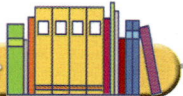

1. What is the athan?
2. Why do we say the athan?
3. What is the iqamah?
4. Would you like to learn the athan?

Word Watch

Athan — أذان
Mu'athin — مُؤَذِّنْ
Iqamah — إقامَة

What is the "Athan"?

Athan is the call for prayer. It is a reminder for people to get ready and come to the masjid for salah. It also makes people remember Allah.

Do you know who a "mu'athin" is?

A **mu'athin** is a person who calls athan. His job is to remind people to get ready for salah. He calls athan five times a day in a loud voice. A long time ago the **mu'athin** used to climb to the top of the minaret or the roof of the masjid, and do the athan there.

A **minaret** is a special tower of the masjid that is made for athan. This way every one around the masjid will hear the mu'athin and know that the salah time has started. Today, most masajid have microphones and loudspeakers, so the mu'athin does the athan into the microphone in the masjid. His voice can be heard around the masjid through the loudspeakers.

When the mu'athin is saying the athan, he faces the qiblah, and raises his hands to his ears.

It has been done this way from the time of the Prophet ﷺ.
We Muslims follow the way taught by him in all parts of our religion.

Bilal ibn Rabah
was the first mu'athin ever!

Bilal's First Athan

Bilal loved to go to the masjid with his father for prayer. Bilal liked to hear the athan in the masjid. "Would you show me how to make the athan, Dad?" asked Bilal. "Of course son," said Bilal's dad. Bilal began learning the meaning of the words of athan. And every day he memorized a few lines of it.

UNIT D CHAPTER 1

One day, Bilal went to the masjid with his dad. He was waiting with his dad for the athan to be made. The Imam saw Bilal and called to him:

Imam: Assalamu Alaykum. What is your name son?
Bilal: Wa Alaykum Assalam. My name is Bilal.
Imam: Masha Allah, your name is like the name of Bilal Ibn Rabah, the first mu'athin in Islam. Would you like to be a Mu'athin like him?
Bilal: Yes.
Imam: Do you know how to say the athan?
Bilal: Yes, my dad taught me that last week.
Imam: Great, would you like to say it now?
Bilal was surprised; he looked at his dad to see what he should do. His dad smiled and nodded.
Bilal: Yes, I will do it, but I might make some mistakes.
Imam: That is all right, son. I will correct you if you do.

Bilal stood and faced the qiblah. He was nervous, because it was his first time to make the athan in the masjid.

Bilal raised his hands to his ears and started to make the athan. Every time he said a verse, the imam and the people in the masjid would repeat the same verse after him in a low voice. The imam kept saying, "Masha Allah, go on Bilal, you are doing just fine." Bilal made only one or two little mistakes, which the imam corrected. After he finished, the imam and the people made a dua'a of the athan. Then everybody thanked Bilal and encouraged him. One person said, "You have such a beautiful voice, masha Allah." His father was also proud of him. When Bilal and his dad returned home, they told the family what had happened in the masjid. His mom hugged him and everyone was very proud of him.

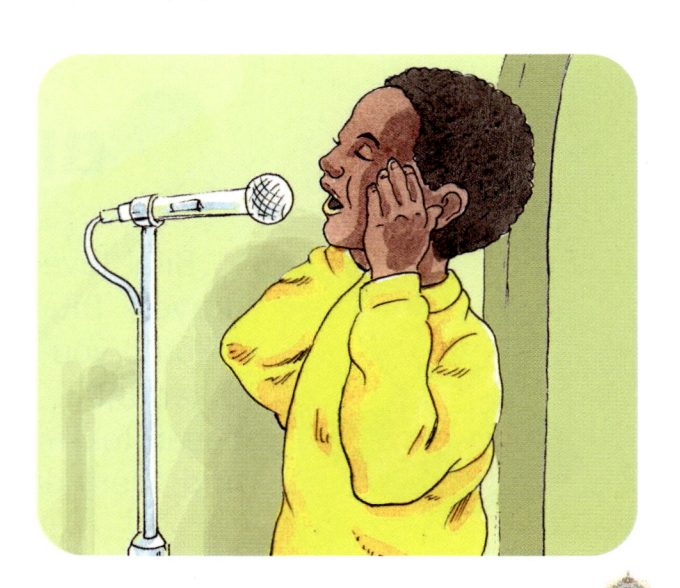

LET US MAKE ATHAN

Would you like to learn the words of athan and their meaning, like Bilal?

اللّه أكْبَر

"Allahu Akbar"
(Allah is Greater) [4 times]

أشْهَدُ أنْ لا إله إلاّ اللّه

"Ash'hadu An la Ilaha IllAllah"
("I witness there is no God but Allah")
[2 times]

أشْهَدُ أنَّ مُحَمَّداً رَسولُ اللّه

"Ash'hadu Anna Muhammada Rasulullah"
("I witness that Muhammad is the messenger of Allah") [2 times]

حَيِّ عَلى الصَّلاة

"Hayyi Alassalah"
("Come to prayer") [2 times]

حَيِّ عَلى الفَلاح

"Hayyi Alal Falah"
("Come to Success") [2 times]

اللّه أكْبَر

"Allahu Akbar"
("Allah is Greater") [2 times]

لا إله إلاّ اللّه

"La Ilaha Illallah"
("There is no God but Allah") [1 time]

D5

UNIT D CHAPTER 1

اللّـه أكْبَر اللّـه أكْبَر اللّـه أكْبَر اللّـه أكْبَر

أشْهَدُ أنْ لا إله إلاّ اللّه أشْهَدُ أنْ لا إله إلاّ اللّه

أشْهَدُ أنَّ مُحَمَّداً رَسولُ اللّه أشْهَدُ أنَّ مُحَمَّداً رَسولُ اللّه

حَيّ عَلى الصَّلاة حَيّ عَلى الصَّلاة

حَيّ عَلى الفَلاح حَيّ عَلى الفَلاح

اللّـه أكْبَر اللّـه أكْبَر

لا إله إلاّ اللّه

THE dua'a OF ATHAN

After the athan is made, Muslims make a du'aa'. They say:

"اللّهم رب هذه الدَّعوة التَّامة والصلاة القائمة آتِ محمداً الوسيلة والفضيلة وابْعَثْه مَقاماً محمودا الذي وعدته"

"Allahumma rabba hathihi-da'wati-tammah wassalatil qa'imah aati Muhammadan al-waseelata wal fadeelah, wab'ath-hu maqaman mahmoodan allathi wa'adtah."

"O Allah, the Lord of this complete religion, and this starting prayer, grant Muhammad Alwaseelah the special and high position in Jannah that you promised him."

What is the "Iqamah"?

The **iqamah** is a fast and short call to prayer. We say it right when we are about to start salah.

What is the difference between athan and iqamah?

The athan and iqamah are very similar. The only difference is after saying "Hayya Alal Falah" you add قَدْ قَامَتْ الصَّلاة "Qad Qamat -is-salah" [2 times]. Which means "Salah has started"!.

Arabic	Times
اللّٰهُ أَكْبَرُ اللّٰهُ أَكْبَرُ	One or Two Times
أَشْهَدُ أَنْ لا إِلٰهَ إِلاَّ اللّٰه	One or Two Times
أَشْهَدُ أَنَّ مُحَمَّداً رَسُولُ اللّٰه	One or Two Times
حَيَّ عَلَى الصَّلاة	One or Two Times
حَيَّ عَلَى الفَلاح	One or Two Times
قَدْ قَامَتِ الصَّلاة قَدْ قَامَتِ الصَّلاة	One Time
اللّٰهُ أَكْبَرُ اللّٰهُ أَكْبَرُ	One Time
لا إِلٰهَ إِلاَّ اللّٰه	One Time

Prophet Muhammad ﷺ taught us to make dua'a between the athan and the iqamah. We should ask Allah ﷻ for his forgiveness at this time. The Prophet told us that Allah will answer the dua'a that is made during that time. Don't waste that special time by talking to your friends!

This is the order of events before prayer:

Athan → dua'a → Sunnah → Iqamah → Salah

WHAT SHOULD WE SAY DURING THE ATHAN?

During the athan, we should repeat what the mu'athin says, except when he says "Hayya Alassalah" and "Hayyi Alal Falah" We do not repeat the same thing. Instead we say:

لا حَوْلَ ولا قُوَّةَ إِلاَّ بِاللّٰه

"La Hawla Wala Quwata Illa Billah"

"There is no strength or power except with Allah"

A TREASURE FROM JANNAH

Did you know that "La Hawla wala Quwata Illa Billah" is a treasure from the treasures of Paradise?

So keep on saying it, and keep on getting rich in good deeds.

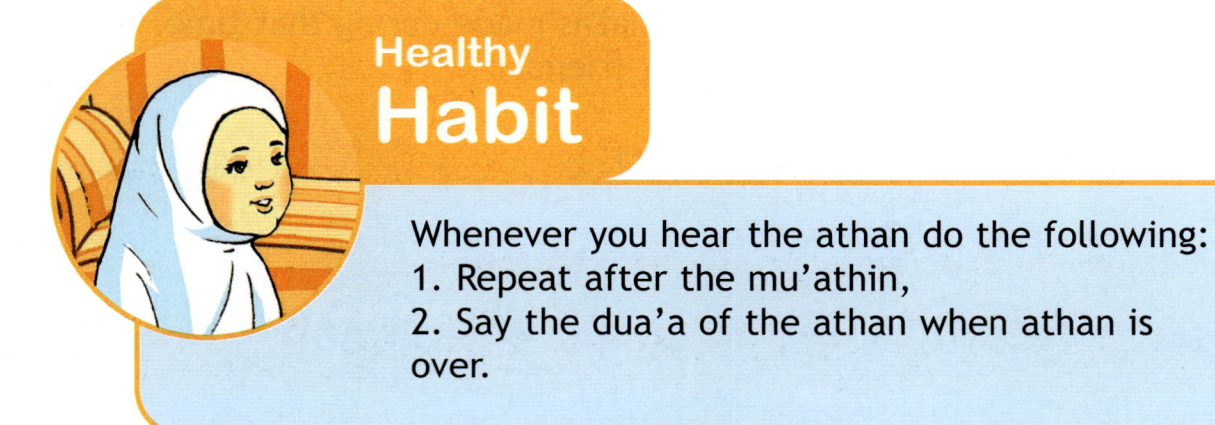

Healthy Habit

Whenever you hear the athan do the following:
1. Repeat after the mu'athin,
2. Say the dua'a of the athan when athan is over.

Chapter Review

Activity Time

Listen to athan on a tape. Then, say athan and iqamah to your teacher and parents.

Think Critically

1. Why do you think athan superior to any other way to call to prayer?
2. How can technology help to make all Muslims hear the athan all the time?

Lesson Review

1. What is the purpose of athan?

2. What is the purpose of iqamah?

3. Say the athan and iqamah, and tell the difference between them.

4. What should you do when you hear the athan?

5. Say the dua'a we should practice after the athan.

UNIT D
CHAPTER TWO
Salat-ul-Jama'ah: A Prayer Allah loves

Pre-reading Questions

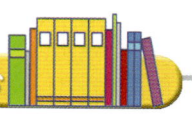

1. What is the importance of Salat-ul-Jama'ah?
2. How do you pray in Jama'ah?
3. Where do we pray Salat-ul-Jama'ah?

Word Watch

Salat-ul-Jama'ah	صلاةُ الجماعة
Qiyam-ul-Layl	قيامُ الليل
Imam	إمام
Ma'moom	مأموم
Ma'moomah	مأمومة

D10

Why do you think Allah ordered Muslims to build masajid? Is it only to pray **Salat-ul-Jumu'ah**, or Friday prayer, once a week? Or only to pray Taraweeh during Ramadan? Of course not. Allah wants us to visit the masjid every day. After all, the masjid is the house of Allah.

Once a blind man came to Rasoolullah ﷺ and said: "O Rasoolullah, I am a blind man, and my house is a little far from the masjid. Could I get permission not to come to the masjid every day?" The prophet ﷺ first said "Yes." The man left, then Rasoolullah quickly called him back and asked him:

"Do you hear athan, the call to prayer?"

"Yes" the man replied. Then, Rasoolullah ﷺ said:

"Then you should answer the call." This means that it is better to come to the masjid for the daily prayers.

Although the man was blind, Rasoolullah wanted him to come to the masjid every day. Why? Because by doing that he earned a lot of reward and blessings. He also learned much more about Islam than if he prays at home.

Later, Abdullah Ibn Ummi Maktoom, the blind man, became a great Muslim. The Prophet ﷺ trusted him and made him a mu'athin. He made the athan in the masjid. Also, Abdullah was sometimes chosen as a leader of Madinah when the Prophet ﷺ was traveling outside the city.

The Prophet ﷺ used to check whether his sahabah came to Salat-ul-Jama'ah or not. He became upset with those who were often absent without good reasons. He understood when they were absent because they were sick or traveling outside of Madinah.

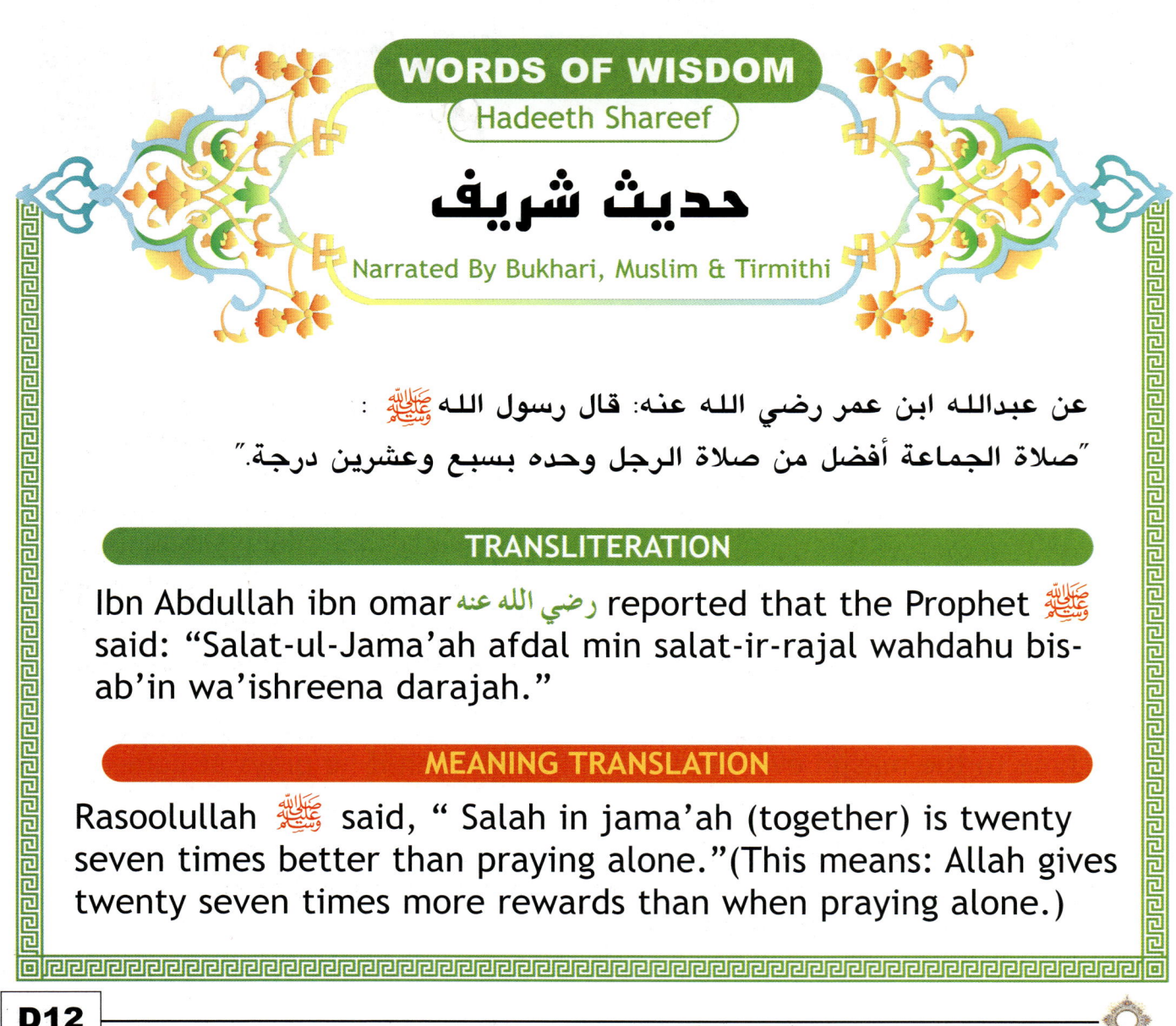

WORDS OF WISDOM
Hadeeth Shareef

حديث شريف

Narrated By Bukhari, Muslim & Tirmithi

عن عبدالله ابن عمر رضي الله عنه: قال رسول الله ﷺ:
"صلاة الجماعة أفضل من صلاة الرجل وحده بسبع وعشرين درجة."

TRANSLITERATION

Ibn Abdullah ibn omar رضي الله عنه reported that the Prophet ﷺ said: "Salat-ul-Jama'ah afdal min salat-ir-rajal wahdahu bis-ab'in wa'ishreena darajah."

MEANING TRANSLATION

Rasoolullah ﷺ said, " Salah in jama'ah (together) is twenty seven times better than praying alone."(This means: Allah gives twenty seven times more rewards than when praying alone.)

Abdullah Ibn Abbas prays Jama'ah with the Prophet

Once, when Abdullah Ibn Abbas was a young boy, he went to spend the night at his aunt Maymoonah's house. His aunt was the wife of Prophet Muhammad. Rasoolullah made wudoo', and prayed four rak'aat then he went to sleep. Later on, a little before Fajr time, Rasoolullah ﷺ woke up again to pray extra prayers for the sake of Allah. This is called **"Qiyam-ul-layl."**

Abdullah watched Rasoolullah praying. He always loved to be close to the Prophet. He wanted a big reward from Allah too. So, Abdullah joined the Prophet and prayed Jama'ah with him.

Shaytan, of course, did not like Abdullah's idea. In fact, Shaytan was very upset to see Abdullah get up, make wudoo', and stand next to Rasoolullah ﷺ to pray Salat-ul jama'ah.

Shaytan became very angry because Abdullah was earning twenty seven times more reward by praying jama'ah than he would have if he prayed alone.

When **Abdullah Ibn Abbas** رضي الله عنه joined the Prophet ﷺ in prayer he made a little mistake. Instead of standing on the right side of Rasoolullah ﷺ, Abdullah stood on his left side. The Prophet ﷺ moved Abdullah to his right side, and they both prayed thirteen rak'aat for the sake of Allah ﷻ.

Abdullah felt very happy. He enjoyed being the **Ma'moom** (follower) while Rasoolullah ﷺ was the **Imam** (the prayer leader).

He learned that one must stand to the right of the imam if there are only two people doing Salatul-Jama'ah.

If a woman is the Ma'moom, she needs to stand behind the Imam.

Rasoolullah ﷺ made a dua'a to Allah to make Abdullah a wise scholar of Islam.

Allah responded to the Prophet's dua'a and **Abdullah Ibn Abbas** became one of the greatest scholars of Islam.

Check Your Understanding

1. What is the name of the young boy who went to sleep at Maymoonah's house?

2. Who is Maymoonah?

3. What did Rasoolullah ﷺ do before Fajr time?

4. What did Abdullah decide to do when he saw Rasoolullah ﷺ praying?

5. Where do people stand when the Ma'moom is:
   One male?
   One female?
   More than one follower?

Chapter Review

Activity Time

Go to the masjid and pray Salat-ul-Jamaáh, then, write a 300 word essay about your experience.

Think Critically

How can Salat-ul-Jama'ah make our Muslim society strong?

Lesson Review

1. What is the name of the young boy who went to sleep at Maymoonah's house?
2. What did Rasoolullah ﷺ do before Fajr time?
3. What did Abdullah decide to do when he saw Rasoolullah praying?
4. What do we call this kind of salah?

UNIT D

CHAPTER THREE

How To Pray Salat-ul-Jama'ah

Pre-reading Questions

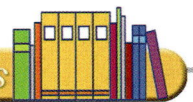

1. Have you been to the masjid before?
2. Did you see how Muslims pray in group?
3. How is Salat-ul-Jama'ah different from praying alone?
4. What do we call the one who leads in Salat-ul-Jama'ah?
5. Can women and girls pray in Jama'ah?

Word Watch

Salat-ul-Jama'ah صلاة الجماعة
Salat-ul-Masbooq صلاة المسبوق

Praying Salatul-Jama'ah

Where do we Pray Salat-ul-Jama'ah?

Usually **Salat-ul-Jama'ah** is done in the masjid. The Prophet and the Sahabah used to pray almost every salah in the masjid. However, a Muslim can pray Jama'ah in school, at work, or at home if he has a good reason for not being able to go to the masjid.

When do We Pray Jama'ah?

Muslims pray Jama'ah in the masjid shortly after the prayer time begins and the Athan is called. Muslims pray Salat-ul-Jama'ah in the masjid five times a day.

Who should pray Salat-ul-Jama'ah?

Allah and the Prophet encouraged all Muslims to pray Salat-ul-Jama'ah in the masjid whenever they can. However, women are excused from praying in the masjid, especially if they are busy at home. Praying in the masjid can be hard on mothers and wives, especially if they have small children.

Praying Salat-ul-Jama'ah

1. Where Should I stand?

Usually, the imam stands in the front and middle. The men line up behind the imam, boys line up behind the men. Girls line up behind the boys, and the women are behind them.

UNIT D CHAPTER 3

So this is what you should do: Stand in line and make sure your **line is straight**.

Ma'moom   **Imam**

If there is a **male imam** and **one male Ma'moom**, the ma'moom stands on the right side of the imam. The same thing if there is a female imam and female ma'moomah.

Imam   **Ma'moomah**

If there is a **male imam** and **one female ma'moomah**, the female ma'moomah stands behind the imam.

2. How Should I Follow the Imam?

- Follow the imam in every move that he makes during the prayer.

- When the imam says Allahu akbar out loud, you should say it quietly to yourself.

- When the imam reads the Qur'an loudly, you listen to him. Only read Al-Fatihah and other surah when the imam is silent.

- Make the movements of salah after the imam does them. Just wait a second or two after he has made a move, then follow it. For example, after the imam makes rukoo,' you make rukoo'. Also after he makes sujood, you make sujood. You do not move with him or before him, you only move after him.

- Do not make unnecessary moves, like looking around, scratching your head, or bumping into the people around you. Be calm and concentrate 100% on the prayer.

Do you do that already?

Takbeer!
Give yourself a pat on the back.
Masha'Allah you are very well disciplined in salah!

Salat-ul-Masbooq: What do you do if you miss some rak'aat?

If you came to the masjid late and find that you have missed one or more rak'ah, do NOT worry, and don't run. Just walk calmly in and join the Jama'ah. Join the last line of prayer, so you do not disturb those in front of you, and follow the imam.

When the imam makes tasleem, do not make tasleem. Stand up and pray the rak'aat you missed. You count the rak'aat you prayed with the imam to determine how many rak'aat you missed.

For example,

If you **pray 3 rak'aat** of the asr prayer with the imam, then you know that you missed 1 rak'ah. After the imam finishes his tashahhud and tasleem, you cannot make tasleem. You have to get up and make the final rak'ah as you normally would, then say your tashahhud and then your tasleem.

If you **pray two rak'aat** of the Asr prayer with the imam, then you know that you missed two rak'ahs. After the imam finishes his tashahhud and tasleem, you don't make tasleem, get up and make up the remaining two rak'aat as you normally would, then say your tashahhud and your tasleem.

If you **prayed one rak'ah** of the Asr prayer with the jama'ah, then you know that you missed three rak'aat. Therefore you have to make up these three rak'aat on your own. So, you pray one rak'ah, and then make the first juloos, read the first tashahhud. Then you stand and pray the two rak'aat left, then make second juloos, read the final tashahhud, and make tasleem.

If you **came in during the final sujood or tashahhud**, then you did not pray any rak'ah with the jama'ah. So, you stand up and pray the full four rak'aat of Asr prayer as you normally would do it alone.

If I enter the salat-ul-jamaah in the middle of a rak'ah, how do I know if that rak'ah counts?

If you enter the salah while the imam is in qiyam or even in rukoo', then that rak'ah counts. If you join after the rukoo', like in sujood, or during tashahhud, then you've missed the rak'ah and you need to make it up.

Chapter Review

Activity Time

Role play how to perform Sulat-ul-Jama'ah if the ma'moon was:

1. One male.
2. One female.
3. Group of males and females.

Lesson Review

1 What do you do when you miss one rak'ah in the masjid?

You pray it and you don't do the tasleem with the imam.

2 What do you do when you miss two raka'at of Salatul-Asr in the masjid?

3 What do you do when you miss three raka'at of Salatu-Thuhr in the masjid?

4 What do you do if you came late to the masjid for Salatul-Maghrib and found the imam sitting for the last tashahhud?

UNIT D

CHAPTER FOUR

Salat-ul-Jumu'ah: The Friday Prayer

Pre-reading Questions

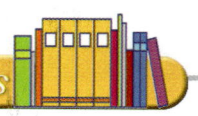

1. What is the most special day of the week for Muslims?
2. What is the special thing that we do on this day?
3. Which prayer is prayed differently?
4. Have you ever been to a masjid on this special day? Talk to your neighbor about what happens there.

Word Watch

Salat-ul-Jumu'ah: Friday Prayer	صلاة الجُمعَة
Al-Jumu'ah: Friday	الجُمعَة
Ghusl: Shower	غُسْل
Khutbah: Speech	خُطْبَة
Khateeb: Speaker	خَطيب

Friday is the most special day of the week for Muslims. The Arabic name for Friday is الجُمعة **Al-Jumu'ah**, which means "the gathering." Al-Jumu'ah is like a holiday. Some people even call it "Eid-ul-Muslimeen," or the "Holiday of the Muslims." In Muslim countries, people usually take Fridays off.

Allah blesses الجُمعات Fridays, and there are many chances for us to earn extra hasanat on these days. There are many special things we do on Fridays. The best and the most important thing Muslims do on Firiday is صلاة الجمعة **Salat-ul-Jumu'ah**, or Friday Prayer. The Friday prayer is a weekly congregational prayer, which means it is done together with the community.

Ghusl on Fridays

It is Sunnah for all of us to take a special bath called غسل **ghusl** on Friday before the Jumu'ah prayer. Ghusl is a purifying ritual. It is like a normal shower, but with some extra steps.

Reading Surat-Al-Kahf

It is also a great thing to recite the first ten ayaat of Surat-al-Kahf on Fridays. The Prophet ﷺ said that whoever recites these ayaat before Jumu'ah prayers will be protected from Ad-Dajjal and the punishment of the grave. And Allah will light up his life that week. The Prophet also recommended reading the whole of Surat-ul-Kahf on Fridays.

Jumu'ah Prayers

Salat-ul-Jumu'ah is the special prayer of Fridays. It takes place at Thuhr time. However, only two rak'aat are performed rather than the usual four. Before the two rak'aat, the Imam gives an inspirational sermon which is called the خطبة **Khutbah**. In it, we learn important lessons about Islam.

The khutbah is a very important part of Jumuah, and we must give our full attention while listening to it. We are not allowed to talk during the khutbah, just as we are not allowed to actually talk during salah. The khutbah is a part of the prayer. A person who gives khutbahs is called a خطيب **khateeb**, even if he's not actually an imam, or, prayer leader.

A person who attends Salat-ul-Jumu'ah regularly will have all the minor sins he/she committed since the last Jumu'ah he/she attended forgiven. Allah has even ordered Muslim men to stop working and go to the masajid during the time of Salat-ul-Jumu'ah. He made it haram, or prohibited, for Muslim men to work or do other things at that time. That is because Salat-ul-Jumu'ah is fard for Muslim men. Only sick people and travelers are allowed to miss Salat-ul-Jumu'ah.

It is the Sunnah of the Prophet to go to Salat-ul-Jumu'ah wearing the best and neatest clothes you have.

Words of Wisdom

Hadeeth Shareef

عن أبي هريرة رضي الله عنه أن النبي ﷺ قال:
"خير يوم طلعت عليه الشمس يوم الجمعة ، فيهِ خُلِق آدَم ، وفيه أُدْخِلَ الجنَّة ، وفيه أُخْرِجَ منها ، ولا تقوم الساعة إلا في يوم الجمعة"
رواه مسلم وأحمد ومالك

Abu Hurayrah narrated that the Messenger of Allah ﷺ said:

"The best day on which the sun rises is Friday. In it Adam was created, entered Jannah, left Jannah, and the Day of Judgment will not happen except on a Friday."

Reported in Muslim, Ahmad and Malik

UNIT D CHAPTER 4

WORDS OF WISDOM
Holy Qur'an

سورة الجمعة

Surat-ul-Jumu'ah 9-11

يَٰٓأَيُّهَا ٱلَّذِينَ ءَامَنُوٓا۟ إِذَا نُودِىَ لِلصَّلَوٰةِ مِن يَوْمِ ٱلْجُمُعَةِ فَٱسْعَوْا۟ إِلَىٰ ذِكْرِ ٱللَّهِ وَذَرُوا۟ ٱلْبَيْعَ ذَٰلِكُمْ خَيْرٌ لَّكُمْ إِن كُنتُمْ تَعْلَمُونَ ۝ فَإِذَا قُضِيَتِ ٱلصَّلَوٰةُ فَٱنتَشِرُوا۟ فِى ٱلْأَرْضِ وَٱبْتَغُوا۟ مِن فَضْلِ ٱللَّهِ وَٱذْكُرُوا۟ ٱللَّهَ كَثِيرًا لَّعَلَّكُمْ تُفْلِحُونَ ۝ وَإِذَا رَأَوْا۟ تِجَٰرَةً أَوْ لَهْوًا ٱنفَضُّوٓا۟ إِلَيْهَا وَتَرَكُوكَ قَآئِمًا قُلْ مَا عِندَ ٱللَّهِ خَيْرٌ مِّنَ ٱللَّهْوِ وَمِنَ ٱلتِّجَٰرَةِ وَٱللَّهُ خَيْرُ ٱلرَّٰزِقِينَ ۝

TRANSLITERATION

9. Ya ayyuhal-latheena amanoo itha noodiya lissalati miy-yawm-il-jumu'ati fas'aw ila thikr-illahi watharol-baya' tha-likum khayrul-lakum in kuntum ta'lamoon
10. Fa-itha qudiyat-issalatu fantashiroo fil-ardi wabtaghoo min fadlillah, wathkurollaha katheeral-la'allakum tuflihoon
11. Wa-itha ra'aw tijaratan aw lahwan-infaddoo ilayha watarakooka qa-ima, qul ma 'indAllahi khayrum-min-al-lahwi waminat-tijarah, wallahu khayrur-raziqeen

UNDERSTOOD MEANING

[62:9] O you who believe! when the call is made for the Friday Prayer, then come quickly to prayer and leave business; that is better for you, if you knew.
[62:10] But when the prayer is ended, then go throughout the land and seek Allah's grace, and remember Allah much, that you may be successful.
[62:11] And when they see business or sport they are drawn to it, and leave you standing [during Khutbah]. Say: What Allah has for you is better than entertainment and business, and Allah is the best of providers.

Story Time

Every Friday, Prophet Muhammad ﷺ gave Khutbat-ul-Jumu'ah, or the Friday sermon, in the masjid. One time a caravan came into Madinah during the Jumu'ah prayer and drove through the streets. One of the people with the caravan was beating his drum and singing. When the people in the masjid heard the caravan coming, most of them left Rasoolullah speaking and went to the caravan to buy goods. Only twelve people, including Abu Bakr and Omar remained and listened to the Prophet's speech.

Prophet Muhammad felt sad that the Sahabah preferred wealth and trade over Salat-ul-Jumu'ah. Allah was not pleased either, so He revealed to Rasoolullah ayaat 9 to 11 of Surat-ul-Jumu'ah. In these ayaat, Allah ordered the Muslims to come to Salat-ul-Jumu'ah on Fridays and leave trade and business at that time. Allah made it haram to miss Salat-ul-Jumuah because of business or other things that are NOT an emergency. If you are traveling, you don't have to pray Salat-ul-Jumu'ah. However, Allah allowed Muslims to trade and take care of their matters before and after this very important salah. It is not a sabbath.

The Special Hour

Rasoolullah ﷺ said that there is a special hour on Friday. During this hour, Allah responds to those who make dua'a to Him. The Prophet ﷺ encouraged Muslims to remember Allah and make dua'a to Him, calling upon Him at that special time. This hour is the hour just before Maghrib, every Friday.

Benefits of Salat-ul-Jumu'ah

Salat-ul-Jumu'ah has many benefits for us, including the following:
1) We obey Allah and please Him.
2) Praying Salat-ul-Jumu'ah will make us earn lots of rewards.
3) All of our sins will be forgiven from one Jum'uah to the next.
4) We are likely to learn great things from the khateeb during the Jumu'ah Khutbah.
5) We stay in touch with our community by attending the Friday prayer. We have the chance to meet new, good people every time we go to the masjid.

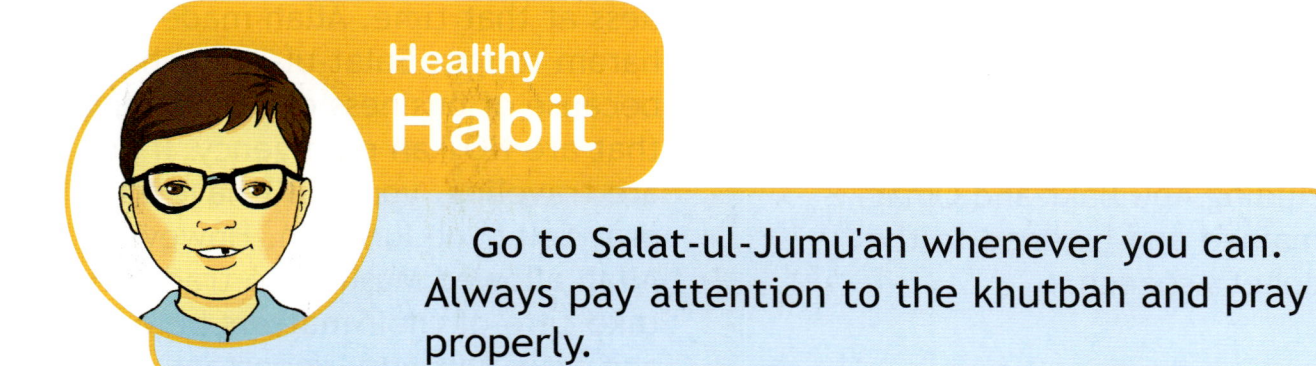

Healthy Habit

Go to Salat-ul-Jumu'ah whenever you can. Always pay attention to the khutbah and pray properly.

Chapter Review

Activity Time

Demonstrate with your classmates how the khutbah and Salat-ul-Jumu'ah are performed.

Think Critically

1. Is Salat-ul-Jumu'ah shorter than normal Thuhr salah?

2. Why do you think the Prophet recommended that we should make ghusl on Fridays?

Lesson Review

1. What day of the week is Jumu'ah? What do we call this day?

2. Name three special things Muslims do on Fridays.

3. What takes the place of the four raka'at normally prayed at Thuhr prayer?

4. What is the Jumu'ah Khutbah? How is this speech or sermon different from other sermons?

5. Can Muslim men miss Salat-ul-Jumu'ah? Why or why not?

UNIT D — CHAPTER FIVE

Appreciating Allah's Gifts

Pre-reading Questions

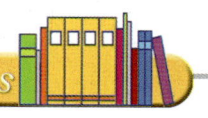

1. Who gave us everything we have?
2. What should we do for the One who gave us everything we have?
3. How can we be grateful to Allah?

Word Watch

- Shukr: Gratitude — شُكْر
- Ni'mah: Blessing — نِعْمَة
- Sujood-ush-Shukr: Prostration of Gratitude — سُجودُ الشُّكْر
- Ma'rib — مَأرِب
- Saba': Sheba — سَبَأ

الحَمْدُ لِلّه

Alhamdulillah

Can you think of how many times in a day you say this word? You say the word at least 17 times in a day! Just think about it. We say Alhamdullilahi rab-il alameen every time we begin to recite Surat-ul-Fatihah for prayer. But why do we say Alhamdullilah so many times?

Look around you. What do you see? You see the many gifts and treasures that Allah has blessed you with. Before you even look at other things, look at your self. Alhamdullilah, Allah has hopefully granted you good health. Hopefully, you can use your two legs to walk and your eyes to see. But these are just some of Allah's wonderful gifts. Allah's gifts are too numerous to count. They include anything that gives us happiness, delight, or comfort such as health, wealth, knowledge, family and much more.

Words of Wisdom

Holy Qur'an

﴿ وَإِن تَعُدُّواْ نِعْمَةَ ٱللَّهِ لَا تُحْصُوهَآ إِنَّ ٱللَّهَ لَغَفُورٌ رَّحِيمٌ ﴾ النحل: ١٨

In Surat-un-Nahl Allah says:

"If you tried to count the favors of Allah, you would never be able to number them; Allah is oft forgiving, most Merciful." [16:18]

How Should We Show Gratitude to Allah?

Sometimes we forget to appreciate the many gifts that Allah has blessed us with. How should we appreciate Allah's gifts? No matter how small the gift that Allah gives us, we must place great value on it and show our appreciation to the Giver. Yes, we need to look beyond just the gift and recognize the Giver, who is Allah ﷻ. We need to do this to express our gratitude and thankfulness toward our great Creator. Expressing gratitude to Allah is an act of worship known as عبادة الشكر Ibadat-ush-Shukr, or the worship of showing our gratitude to Allah. Here is how you show Allah your gratitude:

1. Have a Grateful Heart. You should acknowledge in your heart that everything you have is from Allah.

2. Have a Thankful Tongue. Say Al-hamdulillah with your heart and tongue. Thanking Allah with our tongues means expressing the thanks that our hearts feel. We thank Allah daily by saying Alhamdullilah for the blessings we receive from him such as food, good health, and family. We also thank Allah by our tongues when we say that the gifts and blessings we received are from Allah.

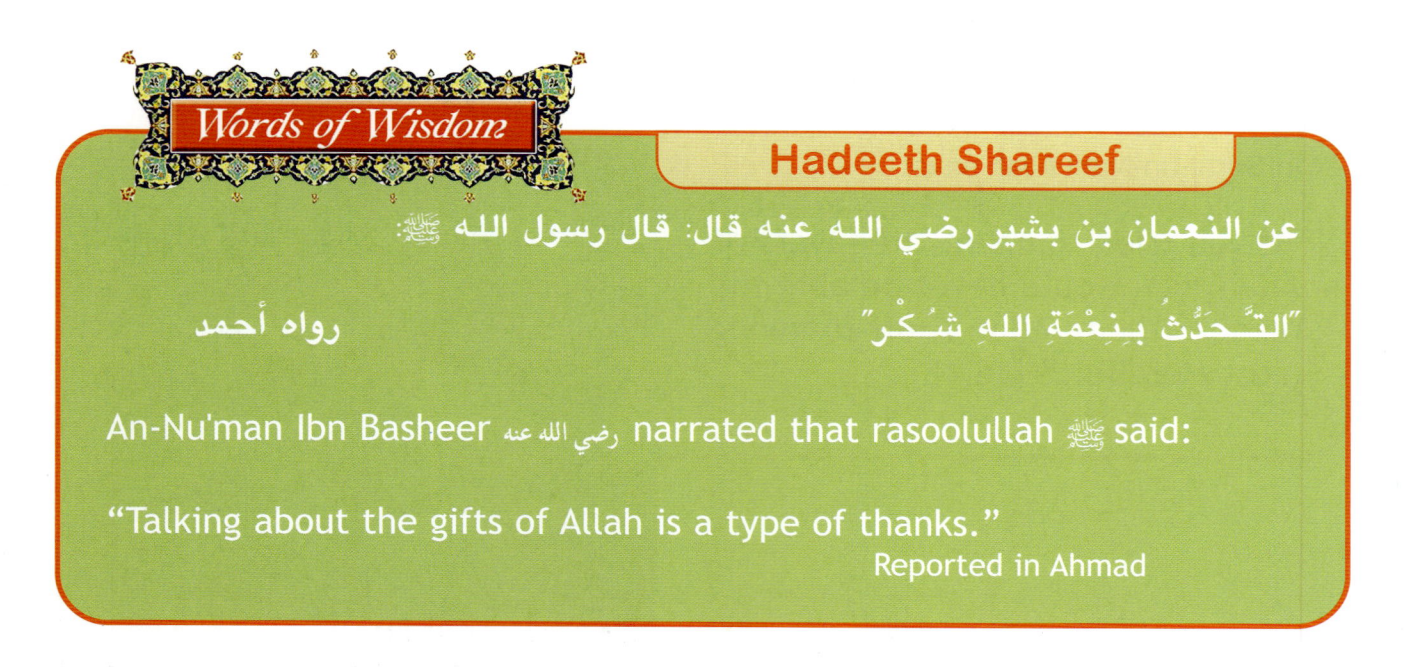

Words of Wisdom

Hadeeth Shareef

عن النعمان بن بشير رضي الله عنه قال: قال رسول الله ﷺ:

"التَّحَدُّثُ بِنِعْمَةِ اللهِ شُكْرٌ"

رواه أحمد

An-Nu'man Ibn Basheer رضي الله عنه narrated that rasoolullah ﷺ said:

"Talking about the gifts of Allah is a type of thanks."

Reported in Ahmad

Words of Wisdom

Holy Qur'an

﴿ وَأَمَّا بِنِعْمَةِ رَبِّكَ فَحَدِّثْ ﴾ هود: ٩٣

"Make the favors of Allah on you known." [93:11]

3. Have a Grateful Body. The Prophet ﷺ sometimes used to stand up in prayer at night until his feet became swollen. Once he was asked why he did this since all his past and future wrong actions had been forgiven. He replied by saying, "Should I not be a thankful servant?" By physically tiring his body the Prophet ﷺ was showing great appreciation for what Allah had blessed him with. One other way to thank Allah is by doing سُجودُ الشُّكْر Sujood-ush-Shukr. Whenever Allah gives you a favor you should make one sajdah, similar to the ones you do during regular salat. In the sajdah, you praise Allah and thank Him for what He did for you.

4. Obey Allah and avoid sins as much as you can.

5. Use the gifts He gave you in the right and halal way. For example, use your eyes to see only good and halal things and avoid using your ears in hearing haram things.

6. Use and consume the gifts Allah gives you properly. Avoid wasting and neglecting these gifts. For example, Allah gave you a beautiful skin, so do not ruin it by applying tattoos or piercing it here and there.

7. Using your energy, time, and money that Allah gave you in serving Islam and helping others.

8. Give sadaqah and charity, if you can, to needy people.

9. If people give you something or help you in a situation, you should thank them and be kind to them. rasoolullah ﷺ said:

" من لا يشْكُر الناسَ لا يشكر الله "
رواه أحمد

"The one who does not thank people [when they do favors for him [or her], he or she is not thankful to Allah."

Reported in Ahmad

UNIT D CHAPTER 5

Shukr or Gratitude Brings You More Gifts and Blessings

Allah loves His servants who acknowledge His blessings and show Him their gratitude. He even gives them more gifts and blessings if they are grateful. Allah says in Al-Qur'an:

﴿ وَإِذْ تَأَذَّنَ رَبُّكُمْ لَئِن شَكَرْتُمْ لَأَزِيدَنَّكُمْ وَلَئِن كَفَرْتُمْ إِنَّ عَذَابِي لَشَدِيدٌ ﴾

إبراهيم: ٧

"And remember! Your Lord declared 'If you are grateful, I will surely give you more, and if you are ungrateful; truly My punishment is terrible indeed.'" [Surat Ibraheem 14:7]

DUA'A

دعاء

عن عبد الله بن غنّام رضي الله عنه قال: قال رسول الله صلّى الله عليه وسلّم:

من قال حين يصبح:

"اللهمَّ ما أصْبَحَ بي مِنْ نِعْمَةٍ فَمِنْكَ وَحْدَكَ لا شَرِيكَ لك. فلَكَ الحمدُ ولكَ الشُّكْرُ"

فقد أدَّى شُكْرَ يَوْمِهِ ومَنْ قال مِثْلَ ذلكَ حين يُمْسي فقد أدَّى شُكْرَ ليلته.

رواه أبو داود

Abdullah Ibn Ghannam reported that rasoolullah ﷺ said: "He who says in the morning " Allahumma ma 'asbaha bi min ni'matin faminka wahdaka la shareeka lak falak-lhamdu walaka-shukr"

Which means: "O Allah, whatever gift I received in the morning is from You Alone, so my praise and thanks are due to you, who ever says this, has rendered his day's gratitude, and he who says the same thing at night has rendered his night's gratitudes.

Reported in Abu Dawood

▲ *Ma'rib in Yemen*

Story Time

Ungrateful Attitude leads to loss of Allah's Gifts

In the Qur'an, there is a story about a people who were a very prosperous nation. They were called Saba' or the Nation of Sheba. They used to live in the area of Ma-rib, in Yemen. They had a great dam called Sadd Ma'rib. The dam was two miles long and 120 feet high. They were very rich and enjoyed a great water supply. The whole area flourished with fruit gardens and was free from insects. The climate was very pleasant. It was a happy country, enjoying canals and roads, and gardens to the right and left.

Each of the twelve towns of Saba' had its own prophet of Allah. Each of the prophets called their people to correct their belief in Allah and obey Him. But the people became arrogant in their wealth, their skills and the great work of their fathers and grandfathers. Sadly, they forgot to praise and worship Allah for all that He had given them. They went astray. So, Allah punished them with a mighty flood that destroyed their dam. Then they lost everything; their dam; their gardens; and their fields. The people of Saba' went from wealth to poverty.

WORDS OF WISDOM

Holy Qur'an

سورة سبأ

Surat Saba' 15-17

﴿ لَقَدْ كَانَ لِسَبَإٍ فِي مَسْكَنِهِمْ ءَايَةٌ ۖ جَنَّتَانِ عَن يَمِينٍ وَشِمَالٍ ۖ كُلُوا۟ مِن رِّزْقِ رَبِّكُمْ وَٱشْكُرُوا۟ لَهُۥ ۚ بَلْدَةٌ طَيِّبَةٌ وَرَبٌّ غَفُورٌ ﴿١٥﴾ فَأَعْرَضُوا۟ فَأَرْسَلْنَا عَلَيْهِمْ سَيْلَ ٱلْعَرِمِ وَبَدَّلْنَٰهُم بِجَنَّتَيْهِمْ جَنَّتَيْنِ ذَوَاتَىْ أُكُلٍ خَمْطٍ وَأَثْلٍ وَشَىْءٍ مِّن سِدْرٍ قَلِيلٍ ﴿١٦﴾ ذَٰلِكَ جَزَيْنَٰهُم بِمَا كَفَرُوا۟ ۖ وَهَلْ نُجَٰزِىٓ إِلَّا ٱلْكَفُورَ ﴿١٧﴾ ﴾

TRANSLITERATION

15. Laqad kana lisaba-in fee maskanihim ayah, jannatani 'an yameeniw-washimal, kuloo mir-rizqi rabbikum washkuroo lah, baldatun tayyibatuw-warabbun ghafoor
16. Fa'aradoo fa'arsalna 'alayhim sayl-al-'arimi wabaddalnahum bijannatayhim jannatayni thawatay okulin khamtiw-wa'athliw-washay-in min sidrin qaleel
17. Thalika jazaynahum bima kafaroo wahal nujazee illal-kafoor

UNDERSTOOD MEANING

[34:15] Certainly there was a sign for Saba' in their homeland; two gardens on the right and the left; eat of the gifts of your Lord and give thanks to Him: a good land and a Forgiving Lord!

[34:16] But they disobeyed, so We sent upon them a flood, and in place of their two gardens We gave to them two gardens producing bitter fruit and (growing) tamarind and a few lote-trees.

[34:17] This is how We rewarded them because they disbelieved; and We only punish the ungrateful.

Chapter Review

Healthy Habits

1. Always remember that Allah is the One who has given you everything in your life.
2. Always have a thankful heart to Allah.
3. Always say Alhamdullilah for the good and bad things in your life. If you suffer bad days, remember the many more good days Allah has given you.
4. Do not look at those who have more than you, but look at those who have less than you.

Activity Time

Make a chart of the many things that Allah has blessed you with. Then make an effort to thank Allah for all the blessings in your life.

Lesson Review

1. How many times in a day do we say the word Alhamdullilah?
2. How can we thank Allah by our hearts?
3. How can we thank Allah by our tongues?
4. Say one dua'a for thanking Allah.
5. Name three other ways that we can thank Allah for the blessings He has provided us with. Give an example for each one.
6. Why did Allah take away the wealth of the people of Saba'?

UNIT D
CHAPTER SIX
Sujood-ush-Shukr

Pre-reading Questions

1. How important is it to appreciate Allah's Gifts?
2. What should we do when something good happens to us?
3. What is Sujood-us-Shukr?

Word Watch

[Sujood-ush-Shukr سُجود الشكر]

There are certain types of sujood that are done outside of regular prayer. One of them is **sujood-ush-shukr** سُجود الشكر . Lets learn together what it is.

One day Bilal and Sarah came home and found their mother very worried. She did not even smile at them as she usually does.

Bilal: What is wrong Mom? Why you are so sad?

Mother: Don't worry about me, let me fix you your meal.

Sarah: Please Mom, tell us what is happening.

Mother: All right, I will let you

know after you eat your meal.

Bilal: Ok Mom, if you insist.

Bilal and Sarah ate their food, washed and brushed their teeth, and then ran to their mother.

Sarah: Tell us now, Mom.

Mother: Your father called me a while ago, and told me that the company he is working in is losing money, and they might lay off a number of employees including your father.

Bilal: So, Dad might be jobless?

Mother: I hope not.

Sarah: That is sad, I pray to Allah to help the company so no one will be laid off.

All: Ameen.

Bilal: Boy, this sounds scary. I never worried about that before. If this happens, Allah forbid, we will be poor.

Sarah: We won't be able to buy the things we like!

Bilal: ...and we won't be able to go on vacations.

Mother: Stop saying that. Just make dua'a and ask Allah to let your father keep his job.

Sarah and Bilal continued making dua'a for their father. In the evening, their father came home and everyone in the house came running around him.

Bilal: What happened dad?

Sarah: Tell us dad!

Father: I don't know yet. We will know by tomorrow, insha-Allah. Don't worry. We will accept whatever Allah chooses for us. He will take care of us, insha-Allah.

Mother: May Allah help us. I am going to fix your dinner.

Father: I want to pray Salat-ul-Asr now.

The family spent the evening thinking and talking about the problem. In the morning, everybody prayed Fajr. Bilal and his father prayed Fajr in the masjid. Sarah and her mom prayed Fajr together at home. They all made dua'a and asked Allah to keep dad on his job. Mr. Mahmood went to work, while Sarah and Bilal went to school.

After school Bilal and Sarah ran home. The moment they got into their house they asked their mother about their father. Their mom said that Mr. Mahmood told her that he didn't learn anything new yet. After a while the phone rang. Mrs. Mahmood answered. Her husband was the caller. Bilal and Sarah listened impatiently.

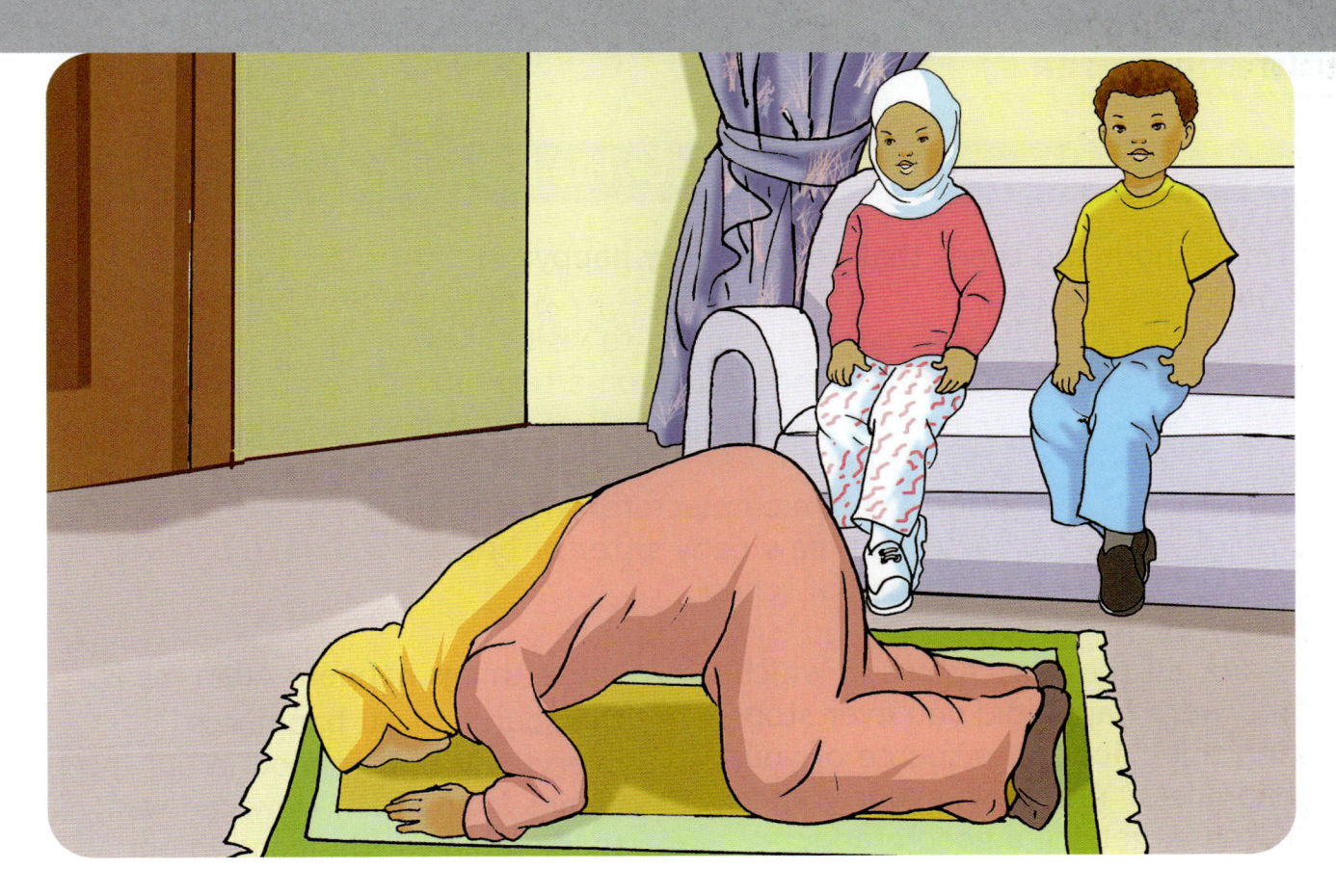

"Al-Hamdulillah, congratulations. We will be waiting for you," mama said happily.

Bilal and Sarah started jumping and laughing. They knew that their father did not lose his job. Mama told them the good news about their father's job. She told them that the company changed their plans and did not fire anyone. Then mama went on and made sujood. Bilal and Sarah looked at each other. Mama took a while in sujood, and then she raised her head.

Bilal: What did you do Mama?

Mama: I made Sujood-ush-Shukr.

Sarah: What is that?

Mama: The Prophet ﷺ used to make Sujood-ush-Shukr whenever something good happened to him. This is one way to thank Allah for His favors. Al-Hamdulillah, Allah kept your dad's job, so I wanted to thank Him by making Sujood-ush-Shukr to Him.

Thanking Allah for His Blessings

Think about the times that you are very happy:

- Grandparents coming to visit
- Getting a good grade on a test
- Fasting the whole month of Ramadan
- Day of Eid
- Going to a nice place for a vacation
- Getting a new baby sister or brother
- First day of school

For all these occasions in which you were happy did you ever stop and think about the source of your happiness? Yes, seeing your grandparents, getting a good grade, enjoying Eid etc. are reasons for you to be happy. However, who permitted these occasions to happen? Who is the One who made all these things happen? Allah ﷻ is the source of all happiness. Everything that is good in our lives comes from Allah. How can we thank Allah for the good in our lives? One way is to do Sujood-ush-Shukur, which is what the Prophet ﷺ used to do.

How to perform Sujood-ush-Shukr

Go into Sujood-ush-Shukr without saying Allah-u-Akbar. Say "subhana rabiy-al-'ala" like you would say during regular sujood. You can also thank Allah and praise Him for the favors He gave to you. When you finish, you raise your head, and no tasleem is needed. You do not need wudoo' to perform Sujood-ush-Shukr, but it is better to do it with wudoo'.

Words of Wisdom

Holy Qur'an

﴿ وَإِذْ تَأَذَّنَ رَبُّكُمْ لَئِن شَكَرْتُمْ لَأَزِيدَنَّكُمْ وَلَئِن كَفَرْتُمْ إِنَّ عَذَابِي لَشَدِيدٌ ﴾

إبراهيم: ٧

And remember! Your Lord declared (publicly), "If you are grateful, I will grant you more (gifts and favors); but if you show ingratitude, truly My punishment is terrible indeed." [14:7]

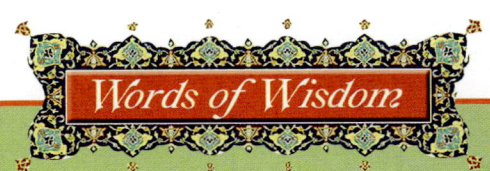

Words of Wisdom

Hadeeth Shareef

عن أبي بكرة الأسلمي رضي الله عنه أن النبي ﷺ "كان إذا أتاه أمرٌ يسرُّه أو بُشِّرَ بِهِ خَرَّ ساجداً للهِ تبارك وتعالى"

رواه ابن ماجه وأبو داود والترمذي

Abu Bakrah Al-Aslamiy narrated that when something good happened to the Prophet ﷺ, or when he received good news, he would make sujood thanking Allah for it.

Reported in Ibn Majah, Abu Dawood and At-Tirmithi

Healthy Habit

Always do Sujood-ush-Shukr whenever something good happens to you or to the Muslims.

UNIT D CHAPTER 6

Did you Know

When Allah helped Prophet Muhammad win over the kuffar of Makkah in the 8th year after Al-Hijrah, he entered Makkah riding on his camel. rasoolullah did not brag or make a victory yell. Instead, he performed Sujood-ush-Shukr on the back of his camel.

Story Time

Once a servant of Allah was making dua'a thanking Allah for His endless gifts. He said:

" يا رَبِّ لكَ الحَمْدُ كما ينْبَغي لِجَلال وَجْهِكَ وعَظيم سُلْطانِك "

Ya Rabbi lak-al-Hamdu kama yanbaghee lijalali wajhika wa atheemi sultanik

"O my Lord, I praise You as your majestic face and grand power should be praised."

The angels became confused. They never heard anyone praise Allah this way before. Therefore, they did not know how many hasanat this servant of Allah should get. His praise of Allah was so great and open ended. Therefore, they went up to the Heavens and asked Allah how they should record these hasanat. Allah then ordered the angels to write the praise of that servant exactly as he said it. Allah promised to reward the man very generously when he meets him on the Day of Judgment.

This is a hadeeth narrated by Ibn Omar and reported in Ibn Majah

Chapter Review

Activity Time

Practice Sujood-ush-Shukr with your classmates.

Think Critically

How does being a thankful person make you a better person?

Lesson Review

1. What is Sujood-ush-Shukr?
2. How do you perform it?
3. When do we perform it? List some reasons.
4. Is wudoo' required for Sujood-ush-Shukr?
5. Write a dua'a you like in which you thank and praise Allah for His gifts.

UNIT D

Zakah: The Third Pillar of Islam

CHAPTER SEVEN

Pre-reading Questions

1. What do you do with your money?
2. Do you give money to the poor?
3. How does a poor hungry child feel when he or she gets money or food?
4. What will happen to you when you give money to the needy people?
5. What is the third pillar of Islam?

Word Watch

Zakah	زكاة
Sadaqah	صدقة
Fard	فرض

﴿ وَءَاتُوا۟ ٱلزَّكَوٰةَ ﴾ الحج: ٧٨

"and give out Zakah."
Surat Al-Hajj 78

Zakah is the third pillar of Islam.
Giving Zakah is **fard**, this means it is required of Muslims.

What does Zakah mean?

Zakah is giving a small part of our savings at the end of each year. Allah commanded us to give to the needy and poor at least 2.5% of our savings every year if they are around four thousand dollars or more. That is one dollar out of every 40 dollars. Allah mentioned zakah many times in the Qur'an. This shows us the importance of sharing our money with those who need it.

Did you know?

IT PURIFIES ME!

When we give Zakah, it purifies our hearts from greed and selfishness.

Story Time

Once Zaid went with his father to the bank. The father took some money from his account, and told his son, "We are going to give this money for zakah." "What is zakah?" Zaid asked.

"It is the money that Muslims must give to their needy brothers and sisters." Answered his father. He continued, "Allah blesses our money and family when we give zakah. Allah (SWT) has promised us that the more we give and share, the more we will receive."

"Does that mean that Allah will put more money in our bank account?" Zaid asked.

"Not exactly that way," answered his father. "Allah blesses our wealth, helps us use it in the best way, and also prevents us from wasting it."

"This tells us," his dad explained, "that the blessings we get from giving zakah are much more valuable than the money itself. And, giving zakah will never make us poor or needy. Allah will always give to us if we remember others. He will reward us with Jannah too"

Zaid learned a lot from his trip to the bank with his father, and said, "When I grow up, I will always pay zakah and give charity to help others."

WORDS OF WISDOM
Hadeeth Qudsi Shareef

حديث شريف

Narrated By Bukhari & Muslim

عن أبي هريرة رضي الله عنه: قال رسول الله ﷺ إن الله يقول:
"أنفق يا ابن آدم، أنفق عليك" رواه البخاري ومسلم

TRANSLITERATION

"Inna Allah yaqool: anfiq ya-bna adam, anfiq 'alayk."

MEANING TRANSLATION

Abu Hurayrah رضي الله عنه reported that the Prophet ﷺ said: "Allah says, "O son of Adam, if you spend (on the needy), I will spend on you.""

Sadaqah: Optional Charity

If we still have extra money after we give zakah, we can give more money to earn more hasanat, or rewards. This extra giving is called sadaqah or charity.

Some people think sadaqah only means giving money. But we can give sadaqah in many other ways if we do not have money.

Here are some other kinds of sadaqah:

1. Smiling at others is a sadaqah.
2. Removing something harmful from the road is a sadaqah.
3. Sharing your lunch with someone who forgot his, is a sadaqah.
4. Picking up litter is a sadaqah.
5. Helping someone carry a heavy load is a sadaqah.
6. Saying a kind word is a sadaqah.

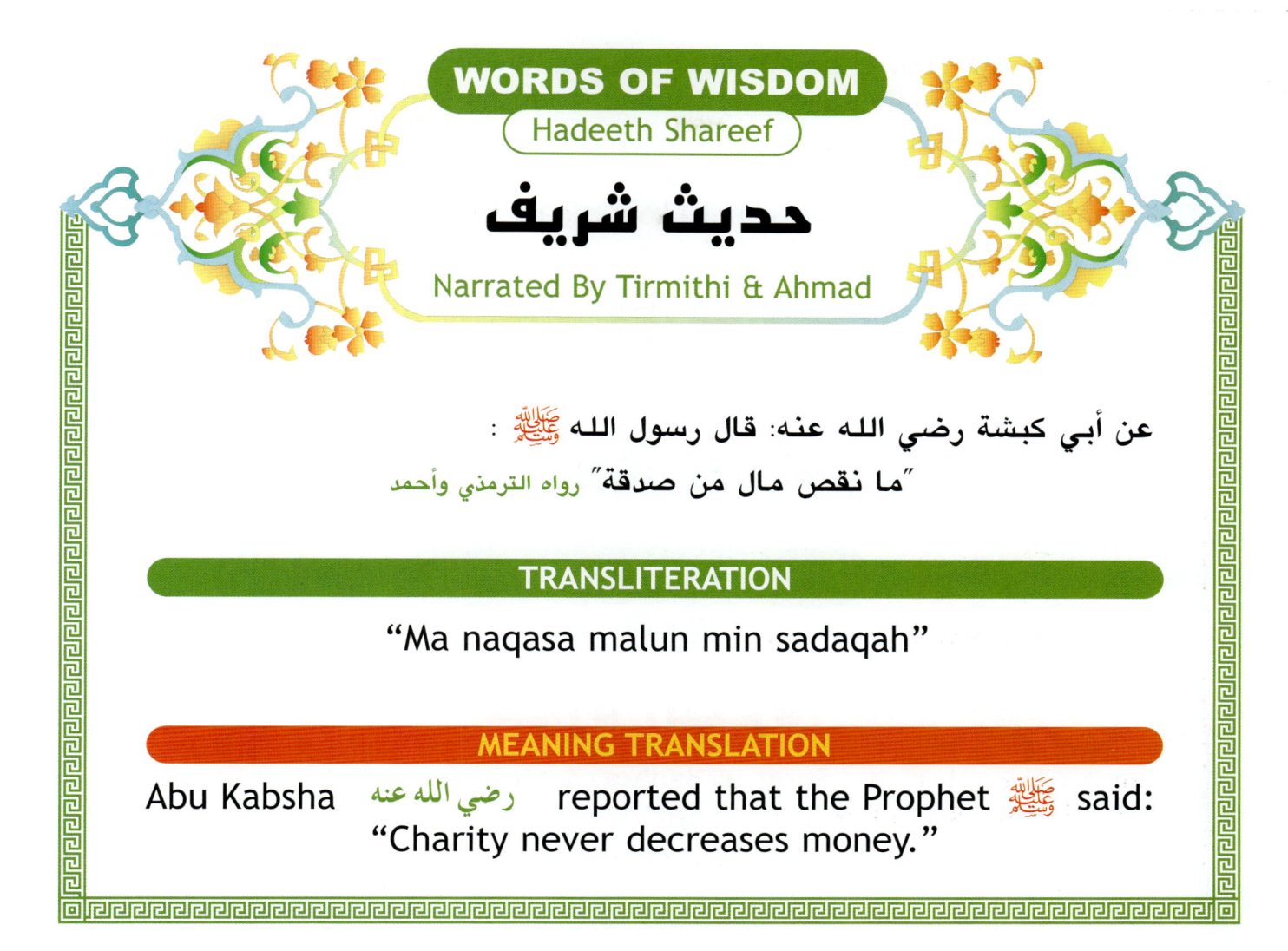

WORDS OF WISDOM
Hadeeth Shareef

حديث شريف

Narrated By Tirmithi & Ahmad

عن أبي كبشة رضي الله عنه: قال رسول الله ﷺ:

"ما نقص مال من صدقة" رواه الترمذي وأحمد

TRANSLITERATION

"Ma naqasa malun min sadaqah"

MEANING TRANSLATION

Abu Kabsha رضي الله عنه reported that the Prophet ﷺ said: "Charity never decreases money."

Did you know when you give charity, Allah ﷻ multiplies it for you on the Day of Judgment. The more you give, the more Allah ﷻ will give you.

Story Time

MY GARDEN BELONGS TO ALLAH!

Once, a person was walking through the fields. Suddenly he heard a voice in the sky: "O clouds, go and rain over the garden of so and so." The voice mentioned the name of the owner of that garden. The man on the ground was surprised. He saw the clouds moving toward a garden so he followed it. A short while after, rain started to fall on that garden. The man was amazed. He looked for the garden's owner and found him. He told him what he heard and saw a while ago.

He asked him: "What do you do so you receive this great care from Allah."

The owner answered, "I do not do much really, Allah is always generous with me. But, I usually divide my income from the garden into three equal parts. One part I spend on my family, another part I spend it on the garden, and the third part I give it to the poor".

The man said, "This explains what I saw today. You are generous, and Allah is more generous with you."

SHARE
GIVE ZAKAH AND SADAQAH

WORDS OF WISDOM
Holy Qur'an

سورة البقرة

Surat-ul-Baqara: Ayah 261

﴿مَّثَلُ الَّذِينَ يُنفِقُونَ أَمْوَالَهُمْ فِى سَبِيلِ اللَّهِ كَمَثَلِ حَبَّةٍ أَنبَتَتْ سَبْعَ سَنَابِلَ فِى كُلِّ سُنبُلَةٍ مِّائَةُ حَبَّةٍ ۗ وَاللَّهُ يُضَاعِفُ لِمَن يَشَاءُ ۗ وَاللَّهُ وَاسِعٌ عَلِيمٌ﴾ (٢٦١)

TRANSLITERATION

"Mathalu-llatheena yunfiqoona amwalahum fee sabeeli-llahi kamathali habbatin 'anbatat sab'a sanabila fee kulli sunbulatim mi'atu habbah, wallahu yuda'ifu limay yasha'o wallahu wasi'un 'aleem"

MEANING TRANSLATION

The example of those who spend their wealth for the sake of Allah is like a grain of wheat growing seven ears. In each ear is a hundred grains. And Allah multiplies for whom He wants; and Allah is all generous, all knowing.

Chapter Review

Think Critically

Some rich people do not give out zakah, while others who are not as rich give zakah regularly. Why?

Healthy Habit

Give Sadaqah or charity to the poor as much as you can.
If you do that you:
- Help your Muslim brothers and sisters
- You help in building strong community
- You please Allah and He will grant you Jannah, inshAllah!

NASHEED

ZAKAH
Listen to this nasheed and try to memorize it.

Lesson Review

1. What is zakah?
2. How important is zakah? Why?
3. When do we give zakah?
4. What is sadaqah?
5. Why does Allah want us to give out zakah and sadaqah?

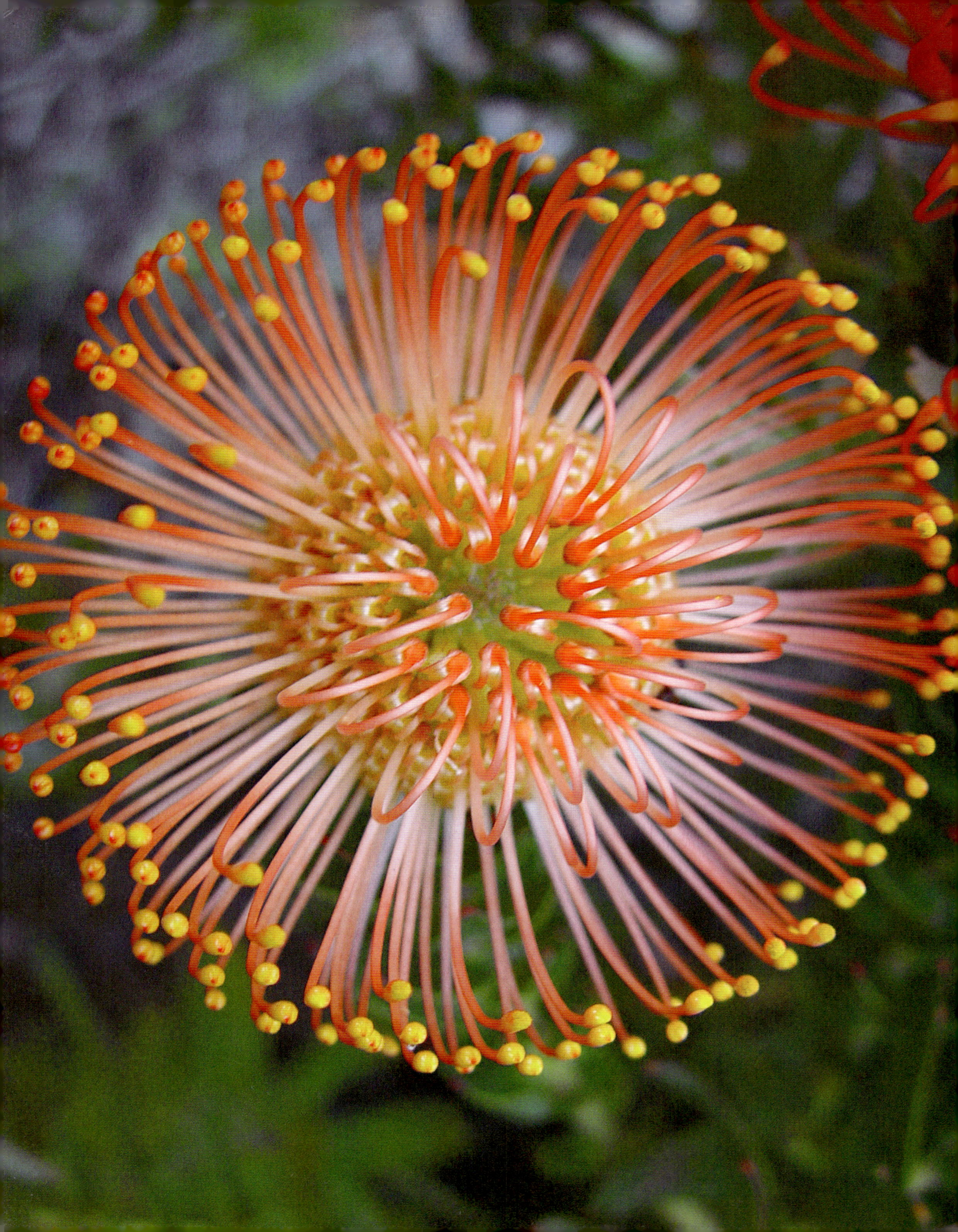

UNIT E

MY ISLAMIC CHARACTER

CHAPTER 1	Brotherhood in Islam	E2
CHAPTER 2	Muslims Love Each Other	E8
CHAPTER 3	The Six Rights of Muslims on One Another	E14
CHAPTER 4	Helping Others, Helping Yourself	E22
CHAPTER 5	I Do Not Hurt Others	E30
CHAPTER 6	Surat-ul-Mutaffifeen	E38
LESSON 1	Surat-ul-Mutaffifeen 1	E38
LESSON 2	Surat-ul-Mutaffifeen 2	E40

UNIT E

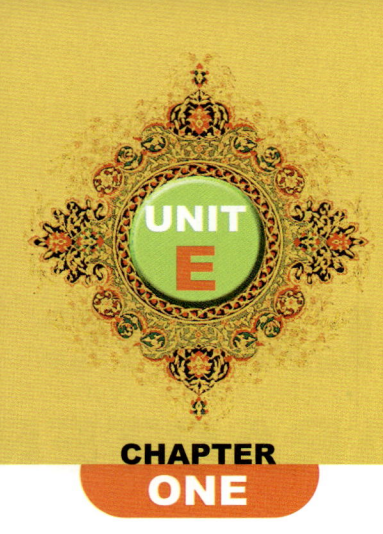

Brotherhood in Islam

CHAPTER ONE

Pre-reading Questions

1. What does brotherhood in Islam mean?
2. Can a brother or a sister in Islam be closer to you than your brother or sister in blood? How?

Word Watch

أخوة	Ukhowwah
المؤاخاة	Al-Mu'aakhah
أخ	Akh
إخوة	Ikhwah
أخت	Ukht
أخوات	Akhawat

﴿ إِنَّمَا ٱلْمُؤْمِنُونَ إِخْوَةٌ ﴾ الحجرات: ١٠

"The believers are but a single brotherhood." [49:10]

Muslims are Your Brothers and Sisters

Islam is not just a religion. It is a way of life. Islam teaches Muslims special ways to deal with each other. In our religion, there is the idea of أخوة ukhowwah, or brotherhood and sisterhood. In Islam, all Muslims are considered brothers and sisters to each other, whether they are related or not. A brother or a sister in Islam can sometimes be better than a real sibling.

Brothers and Sisters in Faith

The Prophet ﷺ taught us that we should admire people according to their devotion to Islam, not merely according to their blood relationship to us. The better Muslim a person is, the more we ought to love him or her. Sometimes a brother in Islam is much more religious and is kinder to you than your own brother or sister. However, we should still love and respect our siblings and relatives, even if they are non-Muslims. Allah and the Prophet ﷺ ordered us to love them and be very kind to them.

Great Examples of Brotherhood

Abu Bakr As-Siddeeq رضي الله عنه was the most beloved companion of the Prophet ﷺ. He was the first man to accept Islam when Muhammad ﷺ became a prophet. Even the Prophet's ﷺ own relatives denied Allah's religion. Abu-Bakr trusted the Prophet ﷺ and did anything and everything he was asked by him to do.

Throughout his life, Abu Bakr As-Siddeeq performed many great deeds. For example, he stayed in Makkah as long as the Prophet did, and helped him make the dangerous trip to Madinah. In his final days, when the Prophet ﷺ was too ill to stand in prayer, he selected Abu Bakr رضي الله عنه from among all the Muslims to lead the prayer for him. Abu Bakr was a true brother in Islam.

Sa'd Ibn Abi Waqqas رضي الله عنه, and Ummu Amarah were among the people who guarded the Prophet ﷺ during the Battle of Uhud. They fought bravely and fiercely against the kuffar to defend the Prophet ﷺ. They cared more about the Prophet ﷺ and his safety than they cared about their own selves.

Talhah Ibn Ubaidullah رضي الله عنه, another sahabi, was a wealthy businessman. He would distribute much of his wealth to the poor. Once, a man seeking charity approached Talhah رضي الله عنه and told him of a distant kinship they shared. Talhah رضي الله عنه was about to sell a piece of land for a large sum of money to someone else. He asked his new relative if he would like that piece of land. But before the relative could reply, Talha asked his relative if he would like to keep the profits of the land, instead. The relative said he would like receiving the profits more, and Talhah رضي الله عنه gave him the money, despite the fact that he had only been introduced to him moments before.

Subhan-Allah, all of the Prophet's ﷺ companions treated their brothers and sisters with the utmost kindness and respect, no matter how closely or distantly they were related.

The Brotherhood between Al-Muhajireen and Al-Ansar

One of the first things Rasoolullah ﷺ did in Madinah, after Al-Hijrah, was Al-Mu'aakhah المؤاخاة. This means that he established a brotherhood between Al-Muhajireen and Al-Ansar. Al-Muhajireen were Muslims who left Makkah for Madinah to practice Islam away from the oppression of the kuffar. Al-Ansar were the residents of Madinah who became Muslims. They received the Prophet and the Muslim Makkans very well. Rasoolullah ﷺ made almost every Muhajir a brother to an Ansari. Al-Ansar took brotherhood very seriously. They invited Al-Muhajireen into their homes and shared their homes, food, and wealth with them. Al-Muhajireen did not have much when they arrived in Madinah, but the Ansar were very generous. Let's read this story:

Story Time

Rasoolullah ﷺ established the bond of brotherhood (Mu'aakhah) between Abdur-Rahman Ibn Awf, who was a Muhajir, and Sa'd Ibn-ur-Rabee', an Ansari. Immediately Sa'd welcomed Abdur-Rahman into his home. Sa'd also told his guest,

"Oh Abdur-Rahman, Rasoolullah made us brothers and you are most welcome in my home. I want to be a true brother in Islam to you. I am going to split my home and money with you; you take half of the home and half of my money too. This way you will be comfortable."

Abdur-Rahman was happy with Sa'd's generous offer. He thought about it a little and said,

"Oh my dear brother Sa'd, may Allah bless you, your family and your wealth. JazakAllahu Khayran for your offer. Please keep your home and money with you. I used to be a merchant in Makkah, and I brought a little money with me. Just show me the way to the market, and I will try to do some business here. May Allah help me."

A few months later, Abdur-Rahman Ibn Awf رضي الله عنه had become a very successful merchant, just as he had been in Makkah. He was a generous man, known for donating money to the Muslims. Abdur-Rahman and Sa'd remained on excellent terms as brothers in Islam until Sa'd رضي الله عنه died as a martyr in the Battle of Uhud, in the 3rd year after the Hijrah.

E5

UNIT **E** CHAPTER **1**

Healthy Habit

Always look for good brothers and sisters in Islam, and try always to be a good Muslim brother or sister to others.

Words of Wisdom

Hadeeth Shareef

عن ابن عمر رضي الله عنه قال: قال رسول الله ﷺ:

"المُسْلِمُ أخو المُسْلِمِ ، لا يَظْلِمُهُ ولا يُسْلِمُهُ ، ومنْ كان في حاجَةِ أخيهِ كان اللهُ في حاجَتِه ، ومنْ فَرَّجَ عَنْ مُسْلِمٍ كُرْبةً فَرَّجَ اللهُ عنه بها كُرْبةً من كُرَبِ يومِ القِيامَةِ ، ومَنْ سَتَرَ مُسْلِماً سَتَرَهُ اللهُ يومَ القِيامَةِ."

رواه البخاري ومسلم

Ibn Omar reported that Rasoolullah ﷺ said:

The Muslim is a brother to a Muslim; he doesn't hurt him nor let others hurt him. Whoever helped his brother when in need, Allah will help him when he becomes in need. And whoever eased a difficulty to a Muslim, Allah will ease his difficulties in the Day of Judgment. And whoever protects the privacy of a Muslim, Allah will protect his privacy during the Day of Judgment."

Reported in Bukhari and Muslim

Chapter Review

Activity Time

Have your teacher start a Pen Pal program with another school. This way you can write letters to other Muslims living elsewhere and make new friends.

Think Critically

Why is brotherhood a part of being a good Muslim?

Lesson Review

1. What does Mu'aakhah mean? And explain the Mu'aakkah that Rasoolullah established.

2. Research a story about how the Sahabah loved their brothers and sisters in Islam. Write a paragraph about it.

3. What are the Arabic words for brother, brothers, sister, and sisters?

4. How is it that sometimes brothers and sisters in Islam can be superior to blood brothers and sisters?

UNIT E

CHAPTER TWO

Muslims Love Each Other

Pre-reading Questions

1. Are there people in your life whom you love a lot?
2. What makes you love them?
3. What does it mean when you love someone?

Word Watch

[Al-Hubbu Fillah   الحب في الله]

Islam is the Religion of Love and Mercy

Allah and the Prophet ﷺ taught us that Islam is the religion of love and mercy. Allah loves us, and one of His names is Al-Wadood, or The Loving. Prophet Muhammad ﷺ loved all the Muslims and all the good people he met. The Sahabah also loved each other and traveled everywhere to guide people to Islam. They wanted all people to go to Jannah because of their love for them.

Allah and His Prophet ﷺ ordered us to love our parents, relatives, friends and neighbors. We are forbidden from hating others or hurting them. In fact, Muslims are even encouraged to be patient with and attempt to win the hearts of those who mistreat them. Allah told us to be kind to them in the hopes that they may change their attitudes.

Love Your Muslim Brothers and Sisters

The first duty we should fulfill toward our Muslim brothers and sisters is to love them for the sake of Allah. This means that we love them to make Allah pleased with all of us. It is important to treat your fellow Muslim brothers and sisters with love and respect, no matter what. All Muslims deserve respect and kindness from each other. It is great to feel love toward your brothers and sisters in Islam, just like you feel love toward your siblings. Love for the sake of Allah is a bond which holds Muslims together.

UNIT E CHAPTER 2

Words of Wisdom

Hadeeth Shareef

عن أبي هريرة رضي الله عنه قال: قال رسول الله ﷺ:
"والله لا تَدْخُلُوا الجنَّةَ حتى تؤمِنوا ، ولا تؤمنوا حتى تحابُوا"
رواه البخاري ومسلم

Abu Hurayrah narrated that the Prophet ﷺ said,

By Allah, you will not enter paradise until you have faith, and you will not have proper faith until you love each other.

Reported in Al-Bukhari and Muslim

For the Sake of Allah

Prophet Muhammad ﷺ said that الحب في الله Al-Hubbu Fillah, which means loving other Muslims for the sake of Allah, is a sign of strong faith. He also said that on the Day of Judgment, Allah will select Muslims who loved each other for the sake of Allah and bring them close to Him. Allah will place them on minor thrones made of light beneath His great throne. Prophet Muhammad ﷺ loved his students and companions very much. They also loved each other. They were a great, big Muslim family.

Story Time

A man named Abu Salim went to visit a Muslim brother called Abu Umayyah. He knocked on the door and a little later Abu Umayyah opened the door.

"Assalamu Alaykum wa rahmatullahi wabarkatuh," Abu Salim said.

"Wa'Alaykum-us-salamu wa rahmatullahi wabarkatuh," Abu Umayyah answered.

"Welcome, welcome, my brother, please come in. I am very happy to see you today."

Abu Salim was happy with the way Abu Umayyah received him. He followed his brother into the house and sat where Abu Umayyah told him to sit. Immediately, the host brought some water and dates for Abu Salim, and said, "How are you, my dear brother?"

"Alhamdulillah, I am fine" Abu Salim replied.

Abu Salim then said to Abu Ummayyah, "Dear brother, I came to visit you at your home for one reason."

Abu Umayyah thought that Abu Salim wanted some help, but he patiently waited until his brother finished his talk.

"I heard Abu Tharr, the great companion of Rasoolullah ﷺ, saying that he once heard the Prophet say: 'If you feel that you love a Muslim brother, then go and tell him.' Abu Salim continued, "And I visited you today just to tell you that I love you for the sake of Allah. I like your manners and the way you treat me and others. I like the way you worship Allah and practice Islam. That is why I

E11

love you for the sake of Allah alone."

Abu Umayyah was touched by these sincere words and thanked his brother in Islam. He told him that he loved him for the sake of Allah, too.

At the end of the visit, Abu Salim and Abu Umayyah hugged. Later the relationship between Abu Salim and Abu Umayyah grew stronger and stronger, and they remained close brothers for life.

How can you Make Others Love and Respect you?

1. Please Allah: If you worship and obey Allah, He will be pleased with you. He will also love you. And when He loves you, he will make people love you too.

2. Be Sincere: When you tell others that you care about them, do not say it unless you mean it.

3. Care and be Kind: If you care about people and treat them kindly, they will like you and grant you their love. Smiles, kind words, and offering to help are all acts of kindness and signs of caring.

4. Give Gifts: People like to receive gifts. Prophet Muhammad ﷺ said,

"تهادوا تحابُّوا"

"Exchange gifts, so you would love each other"

5. Greet Others: People like to be greeted. Rasoolullah once said,

"أَلا أَدُلُّكم على أمرٍ إذا فَعَلتُموهُ تحابَبْتُمْ ؟ أفْشوا السَّلامَ بَيْنَكم"

"Should I tell you about something, [that] if you do it, you will like each other? Spread the greeting of "Assalamu Alaykum" among you."

Chapter Review

Healthy Habit

1. Always love others for the sake of Allah alone.

2. Always treat people with sincerity, care, and kindness so they will love you for the sake of Allah.

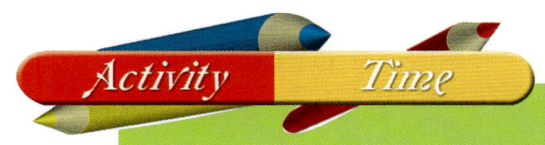

Activity Time

Write the names of the relatives and friends whom you feel that you truly love for the sake of Allah. Then go to each one of them and tell them that you love them for the sake of Allah. You can also call them, write them a letter, or send them an e-mail.

Lesson Review

1 How should you feel toward other Muslims?

2 If a Muslim feels that he or she loves a brother or sister in Islam for the sake of Allah, what should he or she do?

3 How and why is it important to love other Muslims for the sake of Allah?

4 What lessons did you learn from the story of Abu Salim and Abu Umayyah?

5 Is it proper to like people only because they are rich, funny or good-looking? Why or why not?

6 What can make people love and respect you? Give examples.

UNIT E — CHAPTER THREE

The Six Rights of Muslims on Each Other

Pre-reading Questions

1. How should you treat other Muslims?
2. What are some of the rights every Muslim has over every other Muslim?

Word Watch

Haqq حَقّ
Huqooq حُقوق

What is a Right?

A right is something that is due to you from other people, and due to other people from you. In Arabic, the word for "right" is haqq حق . If someone has a haqq on you, then you must fulfill that haqq. If you have a haqq on someone else, then they must fulfill that haqq to you. Muslims have special rights on one another. They are so important that if we do not fulfill the rights of each other, then we can be held responsible for them on the Day of Judgment.

The Six Rights

Prophet Muhammad ﷺ taught us about six special rights of one Muslim on another. These huqooq حقوق , or rights, are very specific. Let's learn about them.

1. Greet Others. Every Muslim you see deserves a greeting. When you meet a Muslim or pass by him or her, you should say "As-Salamu Alaykum." You should also reply to any Muslim who says "As-Salamu Alaykum" to you by saying "Wa Alayikum-us-Salam" or an even better greeting in return. Even if they don't greet you this way, you should still give them salams.

2. Accept Invitations. When you are invited to the house of a Muslim, you should respond and visit. Visiting a Muslim for the sake of Allah is one of the great good deeds a Muslim can do. Of course, you have to have the permission of your parents first.

3. Make du'aa for one who sneezes. When a Muslim sneezes, he or she should say الحمد لله Al-Hamdulillah. Then you should say, يرحمك الله "yarhamuk-Allah." It is the Sunnah to say this, and it means "May Allah have mercy upon you." The person who has sneezed should then say يهديكم الله ويصلح بالكم "Yahdeekum-ullahu wa yuslihu balakum," meaning "may Allah guide you and give you comfort."

4. Give a fellow Muslim sincere and proper advice. We all need help from others, especially in difficult times. Sometimes the help we need is not money, food, or medical treatment, but it might be a wise idea, comforting words, or a solution to a problem. So when you see a Muslim who needs advice, give it to him or her.

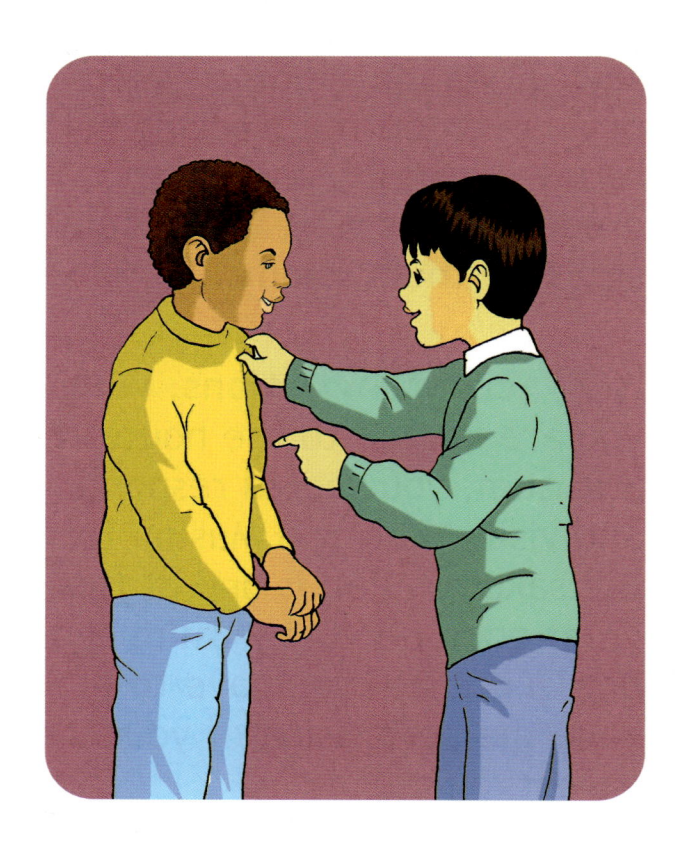

Also when giving advice, make sure that the person really needs it, and that you can really help them. Sometimes you won't have the answer a person needs. In this case, help the person find someone who can help.

Another type of advice you should give is to stop a Muslim from wrongdoing. If you see a fellow Muslim doing something incorrect or bad, tell them about what is right and Islamic, if you know. Remember to follow any advice you give about doing good deeds and avoiding bad deeds.

The Prophet ﷺ taught us the polite and proper way of giving advice. According to him, we should give advice to others in private and NOT in front of other people. We should also say it in a nice, gentle and sincere manner.

5. Visit the sick. Prophet Muhammad ﷺ encouraged Muslims to visit people who are sick. Visiting someone who is ill can help him or her feel better. It also reminds you to thank Allah for keeping you healthy.

6. Attend funerals. Every human being will die one day. When this happens, Muslims must prepare his funeral and bury him with respect. Rasoolullah ﷺ taught us how to prepare funerals, pray for the dead, and perform burials. He also encouraged Muslims to attend funerals, follow processions to the graveyard, and make du'aa'. It is the responsibility of the Muslim community to fulfill this right.

These are all of the general rights that you have on every other Muslim, and that every other Muslim has on you.

1	Greet them with "Assalamu Alaykum."
2	Accept their invitations.
3	Give them sincere advice.
4	Make du'aa for those who sneeze.
5	Visit the sick.
6	Attend funeral.

Words of Wisdom

Hadeeth Shareef

عن أبي هريرة رضي الله عنه أن رسول الله ﷺ قال:
حق المسلم على المسلم ست
قيل ما هنَّ يا رسولَ الله ؟
قال : إذا لقيتَهُ فسلِّم عليه ،
وإذا دَعاكَ فأجِبْهُ
وإذا اسْتَنْصَحَكَ فانصَحْ له
وإذا عَطَسَ فحَمِدَ اللهَ فشمِّتْهُ
وإذا مَرِضَ فعُدْهُ
وإذا ماتَ فاتَّبِعْهُ

رواه مسلم

Abu Hurayra (R) narrated that the Prophet ﷺ once said:

"The rights of a Muslim over other Muslims are six.
He was asked: "What are they, oh Rasoolullah?"
He said: "If you meet him, greet him.
If he invites you, accept his invitation.
If he seeks your advice, give it to him.
If he sneezes, wish him [mercy].
If he becomes ill, visit him.
And if he dies, follow his funeral.

Reported in Muslim

UNIT E CHAPTER 3

Activity Time

In a spacious part of the classroom, lay out plastic cups, pieces of construction paper, or you may subtitute any other small items. Leave enough space in between them for people to walk around. Group up into pairs, with one student in each pair blindfolded. Each pair will take a turn through the "mine field" during which the non-blindfolded partner will guide the blindfolded person through the field using only words. Before passing through the mine field, the non-blindfolded partner must say, "As-Salamu Alaikum (brother or sister), I'd like for you to come to my home." Once the blindfolded partner has made it through the field, he or she responds with "Walaikum as-Salam, thank you for the invitation." Throughout the game, the "home- owner" will advise and verbally guide the blindfolded visitor to protect him or her from the mines and help him get to his home without stepping on any of them.

Mine

Healthy Habit

1. Always give your Muslim brothers and sisters whatever rights they have on you; especially the six rights you learned in this lesson.

2. Always stand by your brothers and sisters. A good Muslim offers help to others even when not asked directly.

Chapter Review

Activity Time

Write a story about Muslims fulfilling the six rights. You may use whatever characters you wish to, just make sure you include all six rights in the story. Be creative!

Think Critically

Why do you think fulfilling the rights of other Muslims upon you is so important?

Lesson Review

1. What is the first thing you should do when you meet or pass by another Muslim?

2. What must you do when another Muslim sneezes and says "Al-hamdulillah?"

3. What should you do when you are offered an invitation to visit a Muslim?

4. If a Muslim gets sick, what should others around him do?

5. What should a Muslim do when a relative or a friend passes away?

UNIT E

CHAPTER FOUR

Helping Others, Helping Yourself

Pre-reading Questions

1. Would you like for someone to help you when you are in need?
2. Can you give examples of times when you have helped others?
3. Does Allah reward those who help others?

﴿ ٱلَّذِينَ يُنفِقُونَ فِى ٱلسَّرَّآءِ وَٱلضَّرَّآءِ وَٱلْكَٰظِمِينَ ٱلْغَيْظَ وَٱلْعَافِينَ عَنِ ٱلنَّاسِ وَٱللَّهُ يُحِبُّ ٱلْمُحْسِنِينَ ﴾ آل عمران: ١٣٤

"Those who give to others in times of ease, as well as in difficult times, and those who control [their] anger and pardon men; and Allah loves those who do good."
[3:134]

WHY SHOULD WE HELP OTHERS

Everyone needs help at some time, in some way. We should be eager to help others, because Allah is pleased when Muslims help each other.

People often need:

Money

Information

Food

Protection

Water

Comfort

Shelter

Ideas

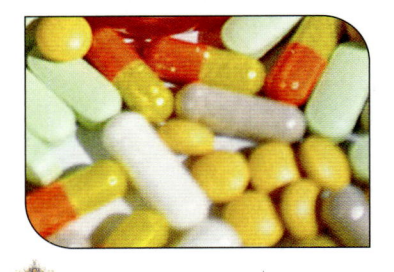

Medicine

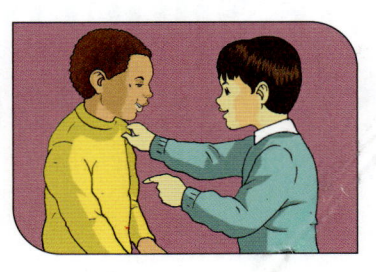

Advice

E23

UNIT E CHAPTER 4

We look to our parents, relatives, teachers, friends and others to provide us with what we need. Even if Allah blesses us with a lot of money, we still need others to help us with different things. We should help others because Allah helps us.

Rasoolullah encouraged Muslims to help those in need. He encouraged his Sahabah to always help and support each other.

Read this discussion between the Prophet and his Sahabah:

> The Prophet ﷺ said:
> "Every Muslim must give sadaqah, or charity."
>
> Sahabah: What if we cannot?
> Rasoolullah: You should work, make money and then give sadaqah.
> Sahabah: What if we cannot work?
> Rasoolullah: Then you should help those who need help.
> Sahabah: What if we cannot?
> Rasoolullah: Then tell others to do good.
> Sahabah: What if we do not?
> Rasoolullah: Then quit doing evil things. That, also, is sadaqah.

WE SHOULD HELP OTHERS SS THE PROPHET ﷺ SAID.

Ways to Help

Helping others is a very important habit that Muslims should develop. A good Muslim loves to help his relatives, friends and others. We can help others in many ways. Giving money, guiding the blind, helping others with carrying their belongings, and/or fixing things are all ways to help others. Having a good attitude towards others also pleases Allah سبحان الله very much.

Helping means standing by your friends in sad and difficult times, helping them understand difficult school work, and helping them solve any problems they may face in their lives.

There are many other things you can do to help others:

- Help your parents with daily chores.

- Visit children in a hospital with your classmates.

- Pick up trash from the road

or the park in your area.

- Hold a door open for someone

- Visit elderly neighbors with an adult and offer them help.

- Help a younger sibling or another child with a homework assignment or project.

- Help someone carrying heavy things.

- If your home has a garden, give your neighbors a bouquet of your flowers or a basket of your fruits.

- Smile!

Helping Others is Good for Us, Too!

When we help others, we actually help ourselves. How is that? When you help others the following things will happen to you:

1. Allah will love you and reward you when you help others.

2. Allah will help you when you need help. Rasoolullah once said:

"والله في عون العبد ما دام العبد في عون أخيه"

"Allah will keep helping his servant as long as he or she helps his brother (or sister)."

3. People whom you helped before will rush to help you when you need help.

4. People love and respect those who are helpful to others.

5. Helping others teaches us many good manners like generosity, mercy, humility, and gratitude to Allah.

Words of Wisdom

Hadeeth Shareef

عن أبي هريرة رضي الله عنه قال : قال رسول الله ﷺ:

"الساعي على الأرملة والمسكين كالمجاهدِ في سَبيلِ اللهِ أو القائِم الليْل الصائِم النهار"

رواه البخاري ومسلم

Abu Hurairah narrated that the Prophet ﷺ said,

"The one who works hard to help the widow and the poor is like the one who fights in jihad for the true cause of Allah سبحانه وتعالى or the one who prays all night and fasts all day."

Reported by Bukhari and Muslim

Small things can make a big difference sometimes.

E27

Healthy Habits

1. Always help others with charity as much as you can.
2. Always give others a helping hand.
3. Always offer others a smile because smiling is charity and it is so easy!

Activity Time

In your home, gather useful things your family does not need that are either brand new or look brand new, such as clothes, toys, food items, etc. Collect these items in a box, and ask your parents to help you deliver them to a poor family, charitable organization or a homeless shelter. Make sure to get permission from your parents before you begin this activity.

Chapter Review

Activity Time

Write a plan to help others and implement it under the supervision of your teacher or parent.

Think Critically

Think of a child living in a poor country. He or she does not have many of the things you do. In a paragraph, compare your life with his or hers. What are some of the things that you have which he or she may not have? How are your lives different?

Lesson Review

1. How important is helping those in need? Why?

2. Name some ways to help others without giving money.

3. How has the Prophet ﷺ helped you?

4. List three helping ideas you learned in this chapter, and three other ideas that come to your mind.

5. How is helping others good for you? List three reasons.

UNIT E

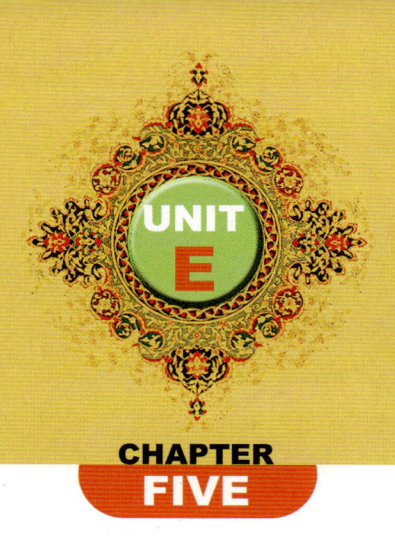

I Do Not Hurt Others

CHAPTER FIVE

Pre-reading Questions

1. Have any of your friends ever hurt you? How?
2. What is gheebah?
3. What is nameemah?

Word Watch

Gheebah	غِيبة
Nameemah	نَميمة
Hisaab	حِساب
Hasanat	حَسَنات
Sayyi'aat	سَيِّئات

Muslims should not hurt each other. They should be good to all people. A good Muslim is kind to everyone around him or her. He or she avoids hurting others or causing them any harm.

How would you feel if someone hit you, pushed you, or ruined your clothes? How would you feel if your classmate lied to you, gossiped about you, or called you names? You would definitely get upset and feel hurt. You might even cry. Allah loves you and does not like for you to get hurt. He also does not like for you to hurt others.

Gheebah and Nameemah

Allah and His prophets made backbiting, gossiping, namecalling, slandering, laughing at others and putting them down all bad deeds. It is haram to do all these evil actions. Lets learn what Allah and Rasoolullah said about these actions.

Words of Wisdom

Holy Qur'an

﴿ يَٰٓأَيُّهَا ٱلَّذِينَ ءَامَنُوا۟ لَا يَسْخَرْ قَوْمٌ مِّن قَوْمٍ عَسَىٰٓ أَن يَكُونُوا۟ خَيْرًا مِّنْهُمْ وَلَا نِسَآءٌ مِّن نِّسَآءٍ عَسَىٰٓ أَن يَكُنَّ خَيْرًا مِّنْهُنَّ وَلَا تَلْمِزُوٓا۟ أَنفُسَكُمْ وَلَا تَنَابَزُوا۟ بِٱلْأَلْقَٰبِ بِئْسَ ٱلِٱسْمُ ٱلْفُسُوقُ بَعْدَ ٱلْإِيمَٰنِ وَمَن لَّمْ يَتُبْ فَأُو۟لَٰٓئِكَ هُمُ ٱلظَّٰلِمُونَ ﴾ الحجرات: ١١

Oh you who believe! Let not (one) people laugh at (another) people perhaps they may be better than they, nor let women (laugh) at another women, perhaps they may be better than the latter. And do not slander each other nor call one another by bad names; evil is a bad name after faith, and whoever does not repent, they are the unjust. [49:11]

﴿ يَٰٓأَيُّهَا ٱلَّذِينَ ءَامَنُوا۟ ٱجْتَنِبُوا۟ كَثِيرًا مِّنَ ٱلظَّنِّ إِنَّ بَعْضَ ٱلظَّنِّ إِثْمٌ وَلَا تَجَسَّسُوا۟ وَلَا يَغْتَب بَّعْضُكُم بَعْضًا أَيُحِبُّ أَحَدُكُمْ أَن يَأْكُلَ لَحْمَ أَخِيهِ مَيْتًا فَكَرِهْتُمُوهُ وَٱتَّقُوا۟ ٱللَّهَ إِنَّ ٱللَّهَ تَوَّابٌ رَّحِيمٌ ﴾ الحجرات: ١٢

Oh you who believe! Avoid suspicion as much as possible, surely suspicion in some cases is a sin, and do not spy nor backbite each other. Would any of you like to eat the flesh of his dead brother? You would hate that; then fear Allah, surely Allah is Forgiving and Merciful. [49:12]

UNIT E CHAPTER 5

Words of Wisdom
Hadeeth Shareef

What is Gheebah?

عن ابي هريرة رضي الله قال : قال رسول الله ﷺ : ما الغِيبَة ؟

قالوا: الله ورسولهُ أعْلَم

قال : ذكرُكَ أخاكَ بما يكرْه

قيل : أفَرَأيْتَ إنْ كانَ في أخي أقول ؟

قال : إنْ كانَ فيه ما تقول فقدْ اغتَبْتَـه وإن لم يكنْ فيه فقد بَهَتَّه

رواه مسلم

The Prophet ﷺ said:
"Do you know what backbiting is?"
The people said,
"God and His Messenger know best."
He then said,
"It is to say something about your brother that he would dislike."
Someone asked him,
"But what if what I say is true?"
The Messenger of God said,
"If what you say about him is true, you are backbiting him. If it is not true then you have slandered him."

Narrated by Muslim

From the above Ayaat and Hadeeth, we learn that gheebah غيبة (backbiting), nameemah نميمة (breaking others' relationships by gossiping), tanabuz تنابز (calling names), and insulting are evil actions.

We Muslims must avoid these behaviors if we want Allah to be pleased with us.

Gheebah and nameemah are evils of the tongue that we might easily commit without thinking about what we are doing, so we should watch what we say. It is wrong to speak ill about anyone, no matter what it is about. A Muslim should not speak badly of someone's personality, looks, character, habits, family and so on. When you speak ill of someone else, you are giving him or her your own حَسَنات hasanat, or good deeds.

Story Time

Rasoolullah once told the Sahabah about a man who was gossiping, backbiting, and slander others. The Prophet said:

"On Yawm-ul-Qiyamah (or the Day of Judgment), Allah will bring that man forth to settle his account حساب (Hisaab). The man will have many bad deeds and very few good deeds. Then Allah will order the angels to take away the man's hasanat and give them to those he hurt. When the hasanat of that miserable man are gone, Allah will order the angels to take the other peoples' سيئات sayyi'aat (bad deeds) and add them to his sayyi'aat.

The man will be left with many many sayyi'aat and no hasanat. Therefore he will be punished in Jahannam, or Hellfire."

To say bad things about someone in his or her absence is called gheebah, or backbiting. Spreading untrue information about someone is called slander. Both are prohibited in Islam.

UNIT E CHAPTER 5

To cause problems between two people or more is called نميمة nameemah. This happens when a person spreads tales among people, trying to make them dislike one other.

If a person is in a situation where others are backbiting, it is his or her responsibility to try to stop the backbiting. He or she should point out the good deeds and qualities of the person the people are gossiping about.

Shaytan Wants Us To Use Our Tongues For Evil

Shaytan always tries to create problems between people. He tempts Muslims to engage in gheebah, nameemah, and other evil actions towards others. Shaytan wants to split Muslims apart by making them hurt and hate each other. Allah ﷻ says:

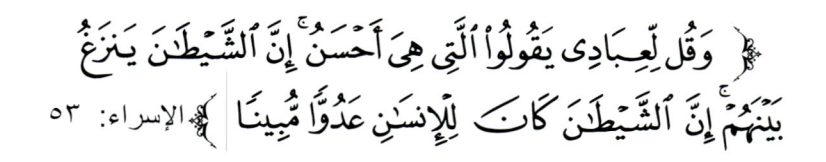

﴿ وَقُل لِّعِبَادِى يَقُولُوا۟ ٱلَّتِى هِىَ أَحْسَنُ ۚ إِنَّ ٱلشَّيْطَـٰنَ يَنزَغُ بَيْنَهُمْ ۚ إِنَّ ٱلشَّيْطَـٰنَ كَانَ لِلْإِنسَـٰنِ عَدُوًّا مُّبِينًا ﴾ الإسراء: ٥٣

"And say to My servants that they should only say those things that are best; surely Shaytan creates hatred among them; surely Shaytan is a clear enemy to man."
[17:53]

Lying, Breaking Promises and Betraying the Trust are all Haram

As you learned earlier, a Muslim is always honest, truthful and trustworthy. Prophet Muhammad ﷺ was honest and truthful from childhood. He always spoke the truth, kept his promises, and kept everyone's trust. He never told a lie, broke a promise, or betrayed a trust. That's why he was nicknamed "As-Sadiq Al-Ameen." (The Truthful, The Trustworthy).

In Islam, being honest and truthful is not a choice, it is a must. It is a major sin to lie or betray the trust of others. These actions hurt people, cause conflict, and spread bad feelings. Often, innocent people get hurt or even lose their lives because of a lie. Therefore, Prophet Muhammad ﷺ warned that lying, breaking promises and betraying trusts are acts of hypocrisy. Hypocrisy is an evil attitude that may lead to hell-fire.

Words of Wisdom

Hadeeth Shareef

عن أبي هريرة رضي الله عنه قال: قال رسول الله ﷺ :

آية المنافق ثلاث : إذا حدّث كذب ، وإذا وعد أخلف ، وإذا اؤتمن خان

رواه البخاري ومسلم

The Prophet ﷺ said,

The signs of a hypocrite are three: when he speaks he lies, when he makes a promise he breaks it, and when he is trusted with anything, he betrays the trust.

Reported in Al-Bukhari and Muslim

UNIT E CHAPTER 5

Chapter Review

Healthy Habit

Always think before you speak and only say things that are good. Always think about how you would feel if someone were to say the same thing about you.

Activity Time

1. Gossip eventually becomes changed when it is spread from person to person. Let's see how this happens by playing the following game:

All of the students in the class should gather in a circle on the floor. One person whispers a sentence, possibly a piece of information learned in class that day, to the person next to him/her. The whispering continues all the way around the circle (with no alteration, you pass along only what you hear!) until the last person says the sentence out loud. The sentence most likely will have changed from what it originally was, and this is what happens with gossip.

2. Write a paragraph or two about an incident where someone said something bad about you. Describe how you felt when this happened.

Chapter Review

Think Critically

1. How are backbiting, slandering, and gossiping bad for the Muslim ummah?

2. Why do you think it is haram to expose the weakness of a Muslim brother or sister, even if you are speaking the truth?

3. Many people can become sad because of gheebah or nameemah. Who would be made happy by it?

Lesson Review

1. What do gheebah and nameemah mean?

2. What are some ways to avoid backbiting, slandering, and gossip?

3. If you hear someone speaking badly about another person, what should you do?

4. Is it okay to say bad things about others if they are true?

5. What will happen to your deeds (on the Day of Judgment) if you gossip?

Surat-ul-Mutaffifeen 1

UNIT E

CHAPTER SIX

LESSON ONE

WORDS OF WISDOM
Holy Qur'an

سورة المطففين

Surat-ul-Mutaffifeen 1-17

﴿ وَيْلٌ لِّلْمُطَفِّفِينَ ۝١ ٱلَّذِينَ إِذَا ٱكْتَالُوا۟ عَلَى ٱلنَّاسِ يَسْتَوْفُونَ ۝٢ وَإِذَا كَالُوهُمْ أَو وَّزَنُوهُمْ يُخْسِرُونَ ۝٣ أَلَا يَظُنُّ أُو۟لَـٰٓئِكَ أَنَّهُم مَّبْعُوثُونَ ۝٤ لِيَوْمٍ عَظِيمٍ ۝٥ يَوْمَ يَقُومُ ٱلنَّاسُ لِرَبِّ ٱلْعَـٰلَمِينَ ۝٦ كَلَّآ إِنَّ كِتَـٰبَ ٱلْفُجَّارِ لَفِى سِجِّينٍ ۝٧ وَمَآ أَدْرَىٰكَ مَا سِجِّينٌ ۝٨ كِتَـٰبٌ مَّرْقُومٌ ۝٩ وَيْلٌ يَوْمَئِذٍ لِّلْمُكَذِّبِينَ ۝١٠ ٱلَّذِينَ يُكَذِّبُونَ بِيَوْمِ ٱلدِّينِ ۝١١ وَمَا يُكَذِّبُ بِهِۦٓ إِلَّا كُلُّ مُعْتَدٍ أَثِيمٍ ۝١٢ إِذَا تُتْلَىٰ عَلَيْهِ ءَايَـٰتُنَا قَالَ أَسَـٰطِيرُ ٱلْأَوَّلِينَ ۝١٣ كَلَّا ۖ بَلْ ۜ رَانَ عَلَىٰ قُلُوبِهِم مَّا كَانُوا۟ يَكْسِبُونَ ۝١٤ كَلَّآ إِنَّهُمْ عَن رَّبِّهِمْ يَوْمَئِذٍ لَّمَحْجُوبُونَ ۝١٥ ثُمَّ إِنَّهُمْ لَصَالُوا۟ ٱلْجَحِيمِ ۝١٦ ثُمَّ يُقَالُ هَـٰذَا ٱلَّذِى كُنتُم بِهِۦ تُكَذِّبُونَ ۝١٧ ﴾

TRANSLITERATION

1. Waylul-lilmutaffifeen
2. Allatheena itha-ktaloo 'alannasi yastawfoon
3. Wa-itha kaloohum aw wazanoohum yukhsiroon
4. Ala yathunnu ola-ika annahum mab'oothoon
5. Liyawmin 'atheem
6. Yawma yaqoom-un-nasu lirabb-il-'aalameen
7. Kalla inna kitab-al-fujjari lafee sijjeen
8. Wama adraka ma sijjeen
9. Kitabum marqoom
10. Wayluy yawma-ithil lilmukaththibeen
11. Allatheena yukaththiboona biyawm-id-deen
12. Wama yukaththibu bihi illa kullu mu'tadin atheem
13. Itha tutla 'alayhi ayatuna qala asateer-ul-awwaleen
14. Kalla bal rana 'ala quloobihim ma kanoo yaksiboon
15. Kalla innahum 'ar-rabbihim yawma-ithil-lamahjooboon
16. Thumma innahum lasalul-jaheem
17. Thumma yuqalu hathal-lathee kuntum bihi tukaththiboon

UNDERSTOOD MEANING

[1] Woe to the unfair,
[2] Who, when they ask for their due rights from other people, they take them fully,
[3] But when they give others their rights, they do not give them their full rights.
[4] Do they not think that they shall be raised again
[5] For a Great Day,
[6] The day when people shall stand before the Lord of the worlds?
[7] Nay! Surely the record of the wicked is in the Sijjeen.
[8] And what do you know what the Sijjeen is?
[9] It is a written book.
[10] Woe on that day to the disbelievers,
[11] Who disbelieve in the Day of Judgment.
[12] And none disbelieve in it but every sinful one
[13] When Our verses are recited to him, he says: "these are] old Stories."
[14] Nay! Rather, their hearts have rusted because of their bad deeds.
[15] Nay! Surely they shall be taken away from their Lord.
[16] Then most surely they shall enter the burning fire.
[17] Then it shall be said: This is what you disbelieved in.

UNIT E

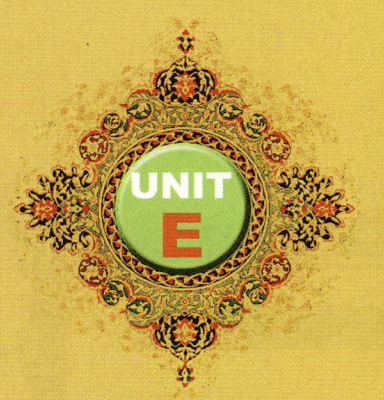

CHAPTER SIX

LESSON TWO

Surat-ul-Mutaffifeen 2

WORDS OF WISDOM
Holy Qur'an

سورة المطففين

Surat-ul-Mutaffifeen 18-36

﴿ كَلَّا إِنَّ كِتَٰبَ ٱلۡأَبۡرَارِ لَفِى عِلِّيِّينَ ۝ وَمَآ أَدۡرَىٰكَ مَا عِلِّيُّونَ ۝ كِتَٰبٌ مَّرۡقُومٌ ۝ يَشۡهَدُهُ ٱلۡمُقَرَّبُونَ ۝ إِنَّ ٱلۡأَبۡرَارَ لَفِى نَعِيمٍ ۝ عَلَى ٱلۡأَرَآئِكِ يَنظُرُونَ ۝ تَعۡرِفُ فِى وُجُوهِهِمۡ نَضۡرَةَ ٱلنَّعِيمِ ۝ يُسۡقَوۡنَ مِن رَّحِيقٍ مَّخۡتُومٍ ۝ خِتَٰمُهُۥ مِسۡكٌ ۚ وَفِى ذَٰلِكَ فَلۡيَتَنَافَسِ ٱلۡمُتَنَٰفِسُونَ ۝ وَمِزَاجُهُۥ مِن تَسۡنِيمٍ ۝ عَيۡنًا يَشۡرَبُ بِهَا ٱلۡمُقَرَّبُونَ ۝ إِنَّ ٱلَّذِينَ أَجۡرَمُوا۟ كَانُوا۟ مِنَ ٱلَّذِينَ ءَامَنُوا۟ يَضۡحَكُونَ ۝ وَإِذَا مَرُّوا۟ بِهِمۡ يَتَغَامَزُونَ ۝ وَإِذَا ٱنقَلَبُوٓا۟ إِلَىٰٓ أَهۡلِهِمُ ٱنقَلَبُوا۟ فَكِهِينَ ۝ وَإِذَا رَأَوۡهُمۡ قَالُوٓا۟ إِنَّ هَٰٓؤُلَآءِ لَضَآلُّونَ ۝ وَمَآ أُرۡسِلُوا۟ عَلَيۡهِمۡ حَٰفِظِينَ ۝ فَٱلۡيَوۡمَ ٱلَّذِينَ ءَامَنُوا۟ مِنَ ٱلۡكُفَّارِ يَضۡحَكُونَ ۝ عَلَى ٱلۡأَرَآئِكِ يَنظُرُونَ ۝ هَلۡ ثُوِّبَ ٱلۡكُفَّارُ مَا كَانُوا۟ يَفۡعَلُونَ ۝ ﴾

TRANSLITERATION

18. Kalla inna kitab-al-abrari lafee 'illiyyeen
19. Wama adraka ma 'illiyyoon
20. Kitabum marqoom
21. Yash-haduh-ul-muqarraboon
22. Innal-abrara lafee na'eem
23. 'alal-ara-iki yanthuroon
24. Ta'rifu fee wujoohihim nadrat-an-na'eem
25. Yusqawna mir-raheeqim makhtoom
26. Khitamuhu miskuw-wafee thalika falyatanafas-il-mutanafisoon
27. Wamizajuhu min tasneem
28. 'aynan yashrabu bihal-muqarraboon
29. Innal-latheena ajramoo kanoo minal-latheena amanoo yad-hakoon
30. Wa-itha marroo bihim yataghamazoon
31. Wa-itha-nqalaboo ila ahlihimu inqalaboo fakiheen
32. Wa-itha ra'awhum qaloo inna ha'ola'i ladalloon
33. Wama orsiloo 'alayhim hafitheen
34. Flyawm-al-latheena aamanoo min-al-kuffari yad-hakoon
35. 'Alal-ara-iki yanthuroon
36. Hal thuwwib-al-kuffaru ma kanoo yaf'aloon

UNDERSTOOD MEANING

[18] Nay! Most surely the record of the pious shall be in the Iliyyeen.
[19] And what do you know what the Iliyyeen is?
[20] It is a written book,
[21] Those who are close (to Allah) shall witness it.
[22] Most surely the pious shall be in bliss,
[23] On thrones, they shall look [around Paradise];
[24] You will see in their faces the beauty of bliss.
[25] They are given a pure sealed drink.
[26] The sealing of it is (with) musk; and for it people should compete.
[27] And the mixture of it is a water of Tasneem,
[28] A fountain from which those close to Allah shall drink.
[29] Surely the guilty used to laugh at the believers.
[30] And when they passed by them, they winked at one another.
[31] And they used to return to their families as winners.
[32] And when they saw the believers, they said: surely these are misguided;
[33] And they were not sent to be responsible over them.
[34] So today those who believe shall laugh at the unbelievers;
[35] On thrones, they will look.
[36] [Now] did the disbelievers get their punishment for what they did?

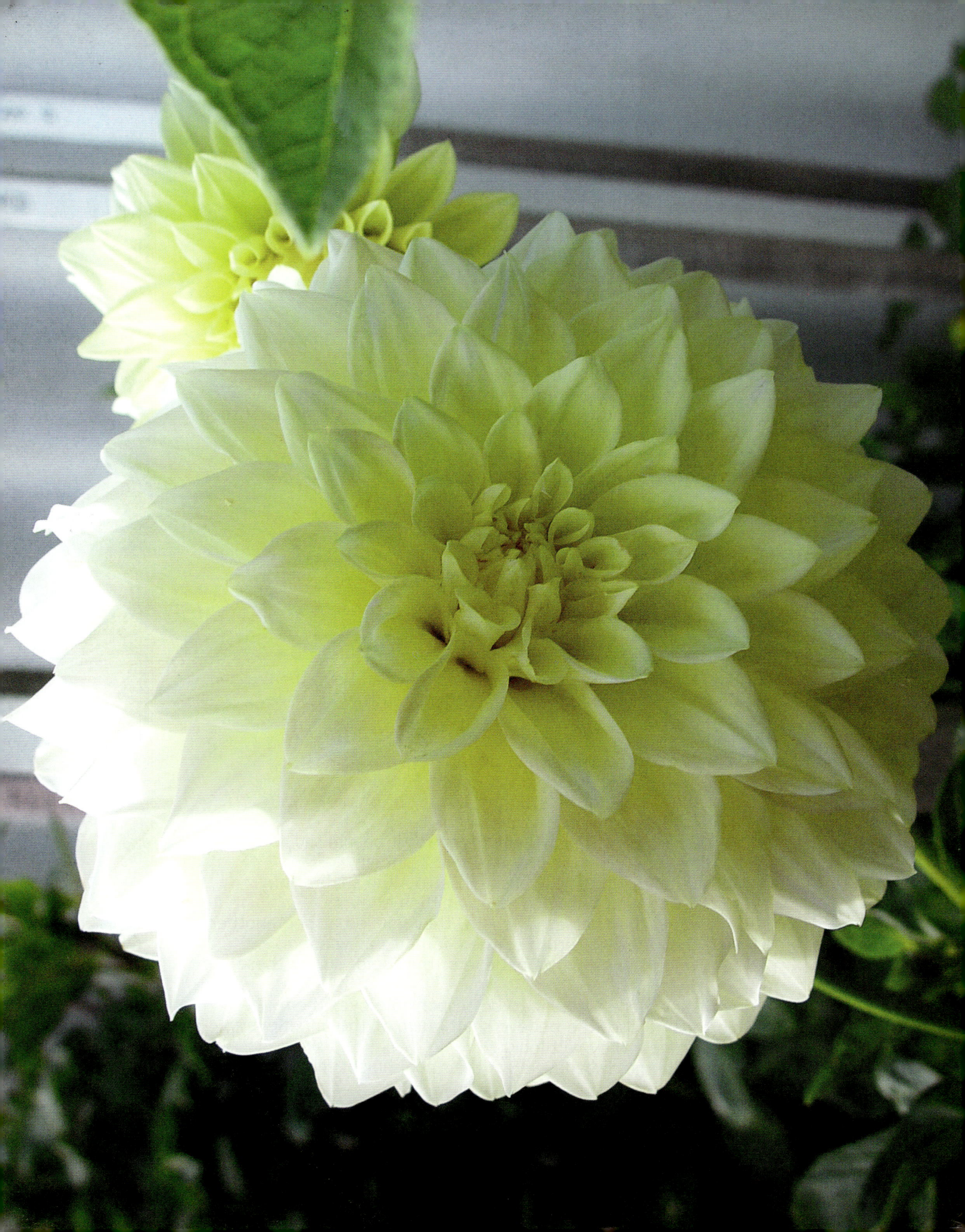

UNIT F

ISLAMIC LIFE STYLE

| CHAPTER 1 | Muslim Fashion | F2 |
| CHAPTER 2 | Muslims Online | F8 |

UNIT F

Muslim Fashion

CHAPTER ONE

Pre-reading Questions

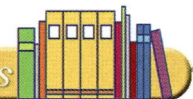

1. What are the important rules for dressing in Islam?
2. Are there different rules for boys and girls?
3. Why is there a "dress code" for Muslims?

Word Watch

Hijab   حِجاب
Hayaa   حَياء
'Awrah   عَوْرَة

Leena Is Dressed For School

Leena looked at herself in the mirror. It was almost time for school, but she wanted to make sure she was dressed appropriately and that her clothes looked neat and presentable.

She had made sure that the clothes she was wearing were clean. As she looked in the mirror, she noticed that hair had fallen out of her hijab. She carefully tucked it back in. Leena knew how important it was for Muslim girls to wear hijaab.

Leena knew that Allah ﷺ and the Prophet ﷺ had made it mandatory for Muslim women to cover their bodies and their hair.

She understood that hijab was not a must on her yet, because she was still young. However, she wanted to start hijab early. This way she wins more hasanat and gets used to it. Leena covered herself in the proper Islamic way because she wanted Allah ﷻ to be happy with her, and she wanted to listen to the Prophet ﷺ out of love.

Leena knew that her hijab was a protection for her, and that it made her personality more important than her looks. She loved wearing the hijab.

Zaid is Dressed For School

Zaid looked in the mirror. He learned from Leena that it was important to check himself before he went out to make sure his clothes were in order. Zaid looked down to make sure his shorts were past his knees. He knew that the Prophet ﷺ had always worn a garment below the knees. He also knew that his 'awrah was from the bellybutton to his knees. Dad had taught Zaid about the 'awrah.

How Can You Dress the Islamic Way

The Islamic dress should meet the following criteria:

1. Covers the 'Awrah

The 'awrah عورة is the part of your body that needs to be covered in front of all people. It is different for boys and girls. For boys, the **awrah** is from the naval, or bellybutton, to the knees. For girls, it is the entire body, except the hands and the face when she is in mixed company. However, when she is with her family or other girls she doesn't need to cover as much.

Even though the 'awrah for boys is from the bellybutton to the knees, this does not mean that boys should walk around without their shirts on. If they need to do something without their shirts, they are allowed to.

Following the rules of 'awrah is mandatory once a child becomes an adult. Still, it is great to practice the rules before we grow up, so that we are used to dressing the right way when the time comes.

Understanding the 'awrah concept is important for us to follow the Islamic dress code. It tells us what parts of our bodies we are allowed to show, and what parts of our bodies we must cover. Covering properly is important because it shows that we have hayaa'. Hayaa', or modesty, is very important in Islam. Modesty means we act in a humble way and that we dress in a humble way.

For girls, another part of covering the 'awrah and maintaining modesty is to not dress in an attractive way. This means that beside covering their 'awrah, the clothes should not be tight-fitting or see-through. Girls should also not wear make up and perfume outside their homes, because this is attractive, too.

Boys should not wear tight-fitting or see-through clothes.

One part of modesty is that we act in a humble way. This means that we should not show off when we wear nice clothes. We should not go out of our way to wear name brands, and if we do, we should not brag about it.

2. Cleanliness

As you learned earlier, cleanliness is half of faith. Muslims must always be clean. The Muslim's body, clothes, home and belongings are always clean. You should avoid getting your clothes dirty. Try your best to keep your clothes clean. If you want to play outside, wear your sports clothes. Also remember, your clothes must be clean inside and out. Some people care about how their clothes look from the outside but neglect their underwear. We sometimes sweat and as a result we get our underwear and outfits dirty and smelly. We should be aware of that and change. Some people use the bathroom and do not clean themselves properly. Muslims should follow the etiquettes of the bathroom properly and clean themselves very well. Being clean keeps you healthy and likeable.

3. Neatness

One day rasoolullah ﷺ spoke about kibr, or arrogance. He advised the Sahabah not to be arrogant. One Sahabi asked the Prophet, "Oh rasoolullah ﷺ ; we like to have neat clothes and look neat, is that a kind of arrogance?" The Prophet ﷺ said, "No, Allah is beautiful and loves beauty." Therefore, a Muslim should be neat. Your shirt should be buttoned, your pants ironed, and your shoe laces tied. You can be neat in different ways, and your parents and teachers are the best ones to know when you look neat and when you don't.

4. Modesty

Being neat and wearing beautiful clothes doesn't mean you have to buy expensive ones. Some people brag about their brand name and expensive outfits. That is unacceptable behavior.

If Allah gave you money to buy expensive clothes, you should thank Allah and avoid talking about it, especially to people who don't have it. You will hurt their feelings if you do that because they cannot afford to buy similar clothes. It is even better not to spend too much money on clothes, shoes or other things. It is better to buy good but inexpensive clothes and give the needy some money to buy clothes for themselves. This will please Allah and make you even happier.

Some people think that if they wear expensive clothes, they will be better than others; that is never the case. What makes you good is not your outfit, it is your manners. Great people are usually modest and hate to brag about their belongings.

Omar Ibn-ul-Khattab used to wear a garment that had many patches. One day his son brought him an expensive garment as a gift. Omar wore the new garment but became restless. He didn't like to wear an expensive outfit while poor Muslims around him didn't have the same. He ordered his sons to bring him back his patched garment to wear. He felt happier wearing the old outfit.

5. Reflecting Islamic Personality

Another thing that we should keep in mind is that when we dress, we should not look to see what styles the non-Muslims are wearing. Many non-Muslims do not cover their 'awrahs, and do not dress modestly.

Instead, we should be creative and think of our own Islamic styles that follow the principles of modesty. We should remember that being neat and presentable is always important.

Chapter Review

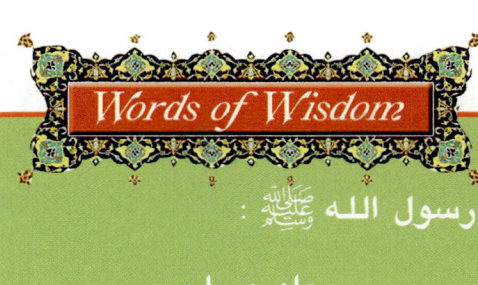

Words of Wisdom

Hadeeth Shareef

عن عبدالله بن مسعود رضي الله عنه قال: قال رسول الله ﷺ:

"إن الله جميل يحب الجمال." رواه مسلم

Abdullah Ibn Mas'oud narrated that the Prophet ﷺ said, "Allah is beautiful and loves beauty."

Narrated in Muslim

Think Critically

1. Why isn't it a good idea for Muslims girls and boys to uncover their 'awrah?

2. Why is it important not to show off about our clothes? What might happen if we do?

Lesson Review

1 What is the meaning of 'awrah? Why is it important?

2 What different things did Zaid and Leena check for in the morning? How did this show they were following the 'awrah rules?

3 Why should we not follow the way non-Muslims dress?

4 What are some rules both boys and girls must follow?

F7

UNIT F

Muslims Online

CHAPTER TWO

Pre-reading Questions

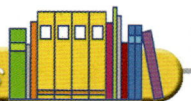

1. How many times a day do you go online? How many times a week?
2. How much time do you spend each day on the internet?
3. What different things do you use the internet for?

Word Watch

Hacker — الشبكة العنكبوتية
World Wide Web
Parental Controls — مراقبة أبوية

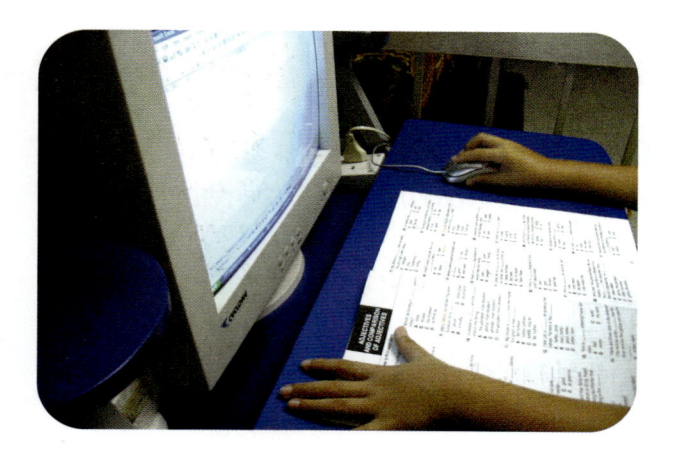

In today's world, the Internet is a very big part of our lives. It is important to remember that the etiquettes that Allah taught us through rasoolullah ﷺ apply to all our actions, even when we're online. If we do this, then even surfing the internet can be a way to worship Allah and get hasanat.

Healthy Habit

Start every session online by saying "Bismillah"

The Biggest Thing to Remember

Even though you may feel like you're all alone when you're online, you and Allah are always close together. Allah knows everything you spend your time on.

Once, Prophet Yaqoob gave a dessert to all of his children and told them to go eat it in a place that no one would see them. All of them went and hid themselves away somewhere to eat their prize happily. It was only Yousuf عليه السلام who came back to him slightly confused. He told his father that

F9

there was no place for him to go to eat where Allah wasn't watching him.

We should remember that Allah is always watching us. He knows what we see, think, hear and say at all times. Remembering that Allah is always watching will help us do good things, while avoiding bad deeds at the same time.

Here are some internet rules to start off with:

1) Make your niyyah: All your work whether online or not should be for the sake of Allah.
2) Look at only what's clean, decent and good.
3) Do not waste your time.
4) Avoid using foul language.

Different things are important to remember whenever we check our e-mail, surf the web, or sign into a chat room.

E-Mail

E-mail, or electronic mail, is a great and fast way for us to communicate. We can stay in touch with our friends and relatives, and we can also communicate to get our work done. Allah likes for us to be close to our families and to do good work, so e-mail can bring us good deeds if we use it properly.

What should we not do with e-mail?

We should not use it to communicate with members of the opposite gender if we do not have a legitimate reason. Girls should not e-mail boys, and boys should not e-mail girls, unless they have a good, Islamic reason to communicate. If you do need to communicate with someone of the other gender, make sure your parents know about it.

A good reason for e-mailing someone of the opposite gender is to get a homework assignment or do some committee work for your Muslim youth group.

We should not communicate with strangers, or anyone we do not know.

Even if we are communicating with someone we know, we should not give out personal information, such as our phone number or address. This is because it is easy for bad people to pretend to be our friends. There are also bad people, called hackers, who break into your computer and take your information.

We should not pay attention to junk mail. This mail either comes from bad people who want to show us bad things, from people who want to sell us items we do not need, or from bad people that want to send us viruses that will mess up our computers. Have a parent, teacher, or other trusted adult teach you how to figure out what is junk mail, and what is not.

Chatting

Chatting online is similar to e-mail, but it is faster and has more instant answers. Chatting is like talking to someone, except you see what they are saying instead of hearing it. It is good to talk to family and friends, as long as we follow the rules.

What should we not do while chatting?

The rules for chatting are the same as with e-mail. We usually should not talk to members of the opposite gender, and never to strangers.

We should not give out our personal information, talk about bad things, or waste our time. It is really easy to lose track of time when we are chatting, so it is a good idea to put a clock near the computer so we can check. We can also set aside a small amount of time to chat. Not wasting time is important, because the time we waste chatting can be better spent doing things that will earn us more hasanat.

The World Wide Web

The World Wide Web, or WWW, is a gigantic place where nearly infinite amounts of information are stored. As with other things, the World Wide Web can be used for both good and bad things.

The best thing we can use the Web for is seeking and gaining knowledge. Allah ﷻ loves for us to learn good things, and using the internet for this reason can give us many good deeds. For example, we may use the internet for projects, papers or just to learn something new. Going on the web is sometimes called "surfing."

We should follow the main rules in the beginning of this lesson about making our niyyah for the sake of Allah, not to waste time, and to only look at good things.

What should we not do on the Web?

Just like with e-mail and chatting, there are bad people on the web that want to hurt our minds and our souls. We should be aware of this, because it is our responsibility to guard our sight.

Therefore, we should not look at anything bad that comes up while we are online, whether it is words, movies, or pictures. A good way to prevent this is to have your parent or teacher put in 'Parental Controls,' which keep most bad things from accidentally popping up. We should understand that 'Parental Controls' are for the protection of our souls. If we need to do something that 'Parental Controls' restrict, then it is a good idea to ask our parents to help us go online.

Overall, the internet can be a great tool for Muslims to communicate, learn and even have fun. It is just as important to remember the rules, because if we don't, the internet can become a very bad thing.

Chapter Review

Activity Time

Make a list of 5 good Islamic websites for kids and share it with your classmtes.

Think Critically

1) Why is it most important to remember that Allah is watching us when we are online?

2) What are some bad things that might happen if we do not follow the rules?

Lesson Review

1) What are the rules that apply to everything we do online?

2) What is another common rule for e-mail, chatting, and web surfing?

3) Why are the rules important and how do they protect us?

I Love Islam - Level 5

INDEX

A

Aad B2, B2, B5, B12
Aaron A8
Abdul Rahman Ibn Awf E5
Abdullah Ibn Abbas D13, D14
Abdullah Ibn Ghannam D34
Abdullah Ibn Jubair C5
Abdullah Ibn Umar Ibn-ul-Khattab C4
Abdullah Ibn Ummi Maktoom D12
Abdur Rahman Ibn 'Auwf C8
Abraham A5
Abu Hurayrah A41, D48
Abu Kabsha A49
Abu- Sufyan C3
Abu-Bakr D27
Abu-Bakr As-Siddeeq E3
Abu-Dardaa' C18
Abu-Dujanah C5, C8
Abu-Salim E10
Abu-Sufyan C8
Abu-Umayyah E12
Accept Invitations E15
Account E33
Adam A4
Ad-Dajjal D23
Admire E3
Advice E16
Ad-Wadood A40
Ahadeeth Shareefah A28
Akh E2
Akhawat E2
Al Khusoo' D2
Al-Ansar E4
Al-Baqee' C16
Al-Bara' Ibn 'Azib C4
Al-Fatihah D19
Al-Hamdullilah E016
Alhamdullilah rab-il alameen D31
Al-Hubbu Fillah E8, E10
Al-Injeel A20
Al-Jumu'ah D20
Al-Kareem A39
Al-khaliq A25
Allah's Gifts D30
Allahu Akbar D5

Allahu Akbar D5
All-hearing B39
Alms A26
Al-Mu'aakhah E2, E4
Al-Mughni B3
Al-Muhajireen E4
Al-Qawiyy A29
Al-Qawiyy A39
Al-Quran A7, A18
Al-Wadood E8
Al-Yasa' A8
Ammouriyyah C14
Amr Ibn Hazm C4
Amr idn-ul-As B9
Anbiyaa' A12
Animals A26, A36
An-Nafi A39
Anxiety A41
Appreciation D32, D33
Ar-Rahman A39
Ar-Riyaa' A32, A37
Asadu Allah C7
Ashamed B25
Ash'hadu An la Ilaha IllAllah D5
Ash'hadu Anna Muhammada Rasullullah D5
Ash-Shirk-ul-Asghar A36, A39
Asia B9
Asiah A5
Asmaa'-ul-Husna A39
As-sadiq Al-Ameen E35
As-Samee' B39
As-Suhuf A20
Athan D2, D7
Athena A34
Attacked B25
At-Tahreef A40
At-Tasbeeh A40
At-Tawrah A20, A44
Attitude E25
Attractive F4
Attributes A29, A39
Awrah F2
Awrah F4
Ayyoob A8

I Love Islam - Level 5 — INDEX

B
Backbiting E31
Bad deeds E31, E33
Battle C4
Belief in One Creator A24
Believing A22
Bellybutton F3
Benefits D28
Betraying E35
Bible A20
Bilal Ibn Rabah D3
Blessing D30
Blind man D11, D12
Bowing A36
Breaking Promises E35
Brotherhood E3
Brotherhood in Islam E2

C
Calf A44
Call for Prayer D2
Call to Prayer D7
Calling Names E32
Care E12
Cavalry C5
Challenged B25
Changing meaning A40
Chaos C5
Character B13
Charity C14, C15, C16, E4
Chatting F11
Christianity C14
Christians A35
Clean F10
Cleanliness F4
Comforting E16
Communicate F13
Congregational prayer D23
Controls A34
Convey A16
Creates A34
Creator A6
Creator, the A25
Crucified C14

D
Danger C7
David A8
Dawood A8
Day of Judgement A18, D44, E10, E33
Dead Sea B22, B24, B32
Decent F10
Denying A39
Desert of Sinai A44
Destruction B18
Devils A39
Devoted C8
Dirty F5
Disbelief A24
Disbelieve A24
Disguised B27
Disobedience C2
Disobeyed C5
Distinction A3
Divine A4
Dua'a A27, B38
Dua'a for one who sneezes E16

E
Earthquake B19
Effects of Shirk A40
Eid-ul-Muslimeen D23
Elias A8
E-Mail F10
Empty Quarters B6
Encourage A12
Entertainment A42
Eros A34
Esfahan C12
Eternity A17
Ettiquettes F5
Evil B17
Evil-Spirits A39
Exalted B38
Ezekiel A8

F
False Gods A24
Fard D46
Father A35
Fear A41
Female ma'moomah D18

I Love Islam - Level 5

INDEX

Fighter A29
First Mu'athin D3
Fleeing C5
Forgiven D28
Fortune Tellers A39
Foul Language F10
Friday Prayer D11, D22
Funerals E18

G
Gheebah E30
Ghusl D20, D23
Gift E12
Giver of Wealth B3
Good F10
Good deads D8, E33
Gossiping E31
Grateful D33
Grattitude D30, D32
Grave yard of Madinah C16
Greatest Sin A26
Greeks A34
Greet E12
Guarded E4
Guidance A12, B22
Guiding E25

H
Habit E25
Hacker F8
Hadith Qudsi Shareef D48
Hadith Shareef A4, A28, A30, D12, D25, D32, D43, D49, E6, E10, E19, E27, E32, E35, F7
Hamzah C3, C5, C6
Hamzah Ibn Abdul Muttalib C2
Handsome B27
Haqq E14
Hardworking B2
Haroon A4, A8
Hasanat E30, E33, F3
Hayaa F2, F4
Hayya Assalah D8
Hayyi Alal Falah D5, D8
Hayyi Alassalah D5

Health A42
Healthy F5
Heart of Worship D2
Heaven A18
Hell A18
Hellfire E33
Helpless B28
Hereafter A42
Hijab F2
Hijaz C15
Hijrah C5
Hind C6
Hind bint Utbah C3
Hinduism A34
Hiraa', cave A6
Hisaab E30, E33
Holiday of the Muslims D23
Holy Spirit A35
Home D11
Horoscopes A39
Hud A8, B2
Hud, Surat B5
Humble B14
Huqooq E14
Hypocrisy E35

I
Ibadat-ush-shukr D32
Ibn Qamay'ah Laithie C7
Ibraheem A4
Idolizing A10
Idols A26
Ikhlas A22
Ikhwah E2
Ikramah C5
Ilyas A8
Imam D10, D14
India A34
Industrious B2
Injustice A41
Inspiration A13
Inspirational Sermon D24
Intelligent A6
Iqamah D2, D7
Iram B2

I Love Islam - Level 5 — INDEX

Iraq B34, C14
Isa A4
Ishaq A4, B27
Ismaeel A4, A6
Israfeel B27

J
Jabal Uhud C2
Jahannam E33
Jahiliyyah A33
Jannah B25
Javelin C3
Jesus C14
Jesus Christ A35
Jian C12
Jibreel, Angel A6, B27
Jinn A39
Job A8
John A5
John A8
Jonah A5, A8
Jordan B32
Jordan River B32
Joseph A5
Jubair Ibn Mut'im C3

K
Ka'b Ibn Malik C8
Khadeejah A5
Khaleefat-ullah fil-Ardh A40
Khalid Ibn-ul-Waleed C5
Khateeb D20, D24
Khutbah D20, D24
Kibr F5
Kind E12
Kindness E4
Knees F3
Knowledgable C14
Kufr A22, A24

L
La Hawla Wala Quwata Illa Billah D8
La illaha illAllah A33, D5
Laughed B35
Lie E35

Light B22
Likeable F5
Lion of Allah C7
Loot A8
Lot A8
Loud Voice D2
Love E8
Lowest Point B32
Lut B22, B25
Lut Ibn Haran B24
Lying E35

M
Madain Salih B12
Magian C13
Mahmood Ibn Lubayd A36
Maintains A34
Major Sin A32
make up F4
Male Imam D18
Ma'moom D10, D14
Ma'moomah D10
Mandatory F2
Mankind A26
Ma'rib D30
Ma-rib D35
Martyred C6
Martyrs C9
Maryam A5
Meeting C16
Mercury A34
Mercy B22, E8
Messenger A12
Messengers A12, A14
Migrated C16
Mikaeel B27
Minaret D2, D3
Minor Shirk A36
Mircales A7
Mischief B29
Modesty F4, F6
Monk C14
Monotheism A2, A22, A33
Moral A6
Morality A18
Mountain A44
Mu'athin D2

I Love Islam - Level 5

INDEX

Muhajir E5
Muhammad A4, C3
Musa A4, A6, A44
Mus'ab Ibn 'Umair C4, C7
Muscat B9
Mushrik A32, A42

N
Nabiy A12
Namecalling E31
Nameemah E30, E34
Naqah B12, B15
Nasibeen C14
Nassebah bint Ka'b C8
Nation of Sheba D35
Naval F4
Naynawa B34, B39
Nazwa B9
Neatest D25
Neatness F5
Neglecting D33
Nervous D4
Ni'mah D30
Niyyah F10
Noah A5
Noble A4
Nuh A4, B2, B4

O
Oman B3, B9
Omani Riyal B9
Omar D27
Omar Ibn-ul-Khattab F6
One True God A29
Online F8
Opposite gender F10
Oppression E4
Optional Charity D48

P
Palestine B32
Paradise A18, A42
Parental Controls F8, F13
Patient A6
Pefume F4

People A26
Permission B35
Person who calls D2
Personality F3
Pharoah A44
Phir'oun, wife of A5
Pious A4
Planets A26
Please D28, E12
Polytheism A24, A32
Poor B14
Positive A12
Power D8
Powerful A29, B14, B28
Prayer leader D24
Privately A27
Promise E35
Promised C14
Prophet A12
Prophet Salhi B16
Prosperous D35
Prostration A36
Prostration of gratitude D30
Protect A39
Protection A13, F3
Psalms A20
Punishment B15
Punishment of the grave D23
Purifies D47
Purifying D23

Q
Qad Qamat-is-Salah D7
Qiblah D4
Qiyam-ul-Layl D10, D13
Qualities A40
Qumay'ah Laithi C7
Quraysh C2, C8

R
Ramadan A26
Rasool A12, A14
Rasoolullah C3
Reflecting F6
Required D46

I Love Islam - Level 5 — INDEX

Respect E3, E4
Responsibility A5
Responsible A16
Revelations A18
Revenge C2
Rewards A42
Rewards D28
Rich B14
Ridiculed A6
Righeous A12
Right E14
Romans A34
Roof D2
Rukoo' D19
Rusul A12, A14

S

Saba' D30, D35
Sabbath D27
Sa'd Ibn Abi Waqass C8, E4
Sa'd Ibn ur-Rabee' E5
Sadaqah C16, D46, D48
Sadd' Ma'rib D35
Sadoom B24
Sahabah E24
Saints A26
Sake of Allah E10
Salah has started D7
Salaha B9
Salat-ul-Jama'ah D10
Salat-ul-Jama'ah D16, D23
Salat-ul-Jum'ah D11, D22
Salat-ul-Masbooq D16, D20
Salih A8, B12
Salman Al-Farsi C12
Salman the Persian C12
Saudi Arabia B2, B13
Sayyi'aat E30, E33
Scholars D14
Scripture A20
Scrolls A20
Seal of Prophethood C15
See-through F4
Sermon, Friday D27
Shahadah A22, A33

Shameful B24
Shawwal C5
Sheba D30
She-camel B15
Sheebah E32
Ship B35
Shirk A22, A24, A32
Shirk Al-Asghar A32
Shirk Ar-Ruboobiyyah A34
Shirk in Al-Asmaa' was Sifaat A39
Shirk in Ibadah A36
Shower D20, D23
Showing off A36
Shu'ayb A8
Shukr D30
Sifat A22
Sihr A32
Sincere C14, E12
Sisterhood E3
Six Rights E15
Slandering E31
Slaughtered B17
Smelly F5
Smiles E12
Sodom B22, B28
Sodom B24
Solomon A8
Son A35
Son of Mary C14
Soor B9
Speak Badly E33
Speaker D20
Special Hour D28
Special Rights E4
Speech D20
Storm B7, B36
Strength D8
Strong Leader A29
Suhar B9
Suhuf A20
Sujood D19, D20
Sujood-ush-Shukr D30, D33, D38
Sujood-ush-Shukr, Peform D42
Sulayman A8
Superstitions A41
Supplication A27, A36
Surat Hud 11:53-54 B6

I Love Islam - Level 5

INDEX

Surat Saba' D36
Surat Saba' 15-17 D36
Surat-al-Kahf D23
Surat-ul-Anbiya'a Ayah 87 B38
Surat-ul-A'raaf A12
Surat-ul-A'raf 7:73 B13
Surat-ul-Baqarah: Ayah 261 D50
Surat-ul-Hajj A40
Surat-ul-Ikhlas A23
Surat-ul-Jumu'ah D26
Surat-ul-Jumu'ah 9-11 D26
Surat-ul-Mutaffifeen E38, E40
Surat-ul-Mutaffifeen 1-17 E38
Surat-ul-Mutaffifeen 18-36 E40
Surat-ul-Qamar B8, B30
Surat-ul-Qamar 18-22 B8
Surat-ul-Qamar 33-40 B30
Surat-un-Naba A46, A48, A50
Surat-un-Naba 1-16 A46, A48, A50
Surat-un-Naba 17-30 A48
Surat-un-Naba 31-40 A50
Surat-u-Shams B19
Surat-ush-Shu'araa' 26: 155 B16
Surat-us-Shams B19
Surat-ut-Takweer C20, C22
Surat-ut-Takweer 1-14 C20
Surat-ut-Takweer 15-29 C22
Surfing F12
Sustainer A6
Suwar A22
Swallowed B4
Syria C14

T
Talhah E4
Talhah Ibn Abu-Talhah C5
Talhah Ibn Ubaidullah E4
Tanabuz E32
Tasbeeh B38
Tashahud D20
Tawaaf A36
Tawheed A2, A6, A20, A22
Tawheed-ul-Asmaa'-was-Sifaat A22
Tawheed-ul-Asmaa'-was-Sifaat A29
Tawheed-ul-Ebadah A22

Tawheed-ul-Ibadah A26
Tawheed-ul-Khaliq A22, A24
Tawheed-ur-Ruboobiyyah A24
Testimony A22
Thamood B12
Thankful D32
The Camel, The miracle of B15
The Dua'a of Athan D6
The End C8
The End of the Battle C8
The gathering D23
The Message A10
The Truthful E35
Third Pillar of Islam D46
Threatened B25
Thuhr D23
Thul-kifl A8
Tight-fitting F4
Together D23
Tolerant A6
Torah A20, A44
Tower D3
Towns of Salih B13
Trading Post B4
Trinity A35
True Faith C14
Trust E35
Trustworthy E35
Truth E35
Turkey C14

U
Ubar B2, B4
Ubay C8
Udud, the Battle of C2
Uhud C5, E5
Ukhowwah E2, E3
Ukht E2
Ummu-Omarah C8
Uncle of the Prophet C2
Underwear F5
Ungodly A40
Ungrateful D35
Usamah Ibn Zaid C4